PALERMO TRAVEL GUIDE 2023 AND BEYOND

Immersing Yourself in Sicily's Cultural Hub

By: Alessio Romano

Contents

INTRODUCTION 1

IMPORTANT INFORMATION 3

Basic Information 4

Port of Palermo 8

Accommodation in Palermo 10

FAQ 13

PALERMO HISTORY 16

Ancient Roots and Early Settlers 17

Byzantine and Arab Influences 18

Norman Conquest and Cultural Fusion 20

Spanish Domination and Baroque Splendor 22

Unification of Italy and Modernization 24

Contemporary Palermo 26

HISTORIC DISTRICTS 28

La Kalsa 29

Albergheria 30

Vucciria 33

Capo 35

Kalsa-Marina 37

Palazzo dei Normanni District 38

La Loggia District 40

HISTORICAL SITES AND LANDMARKS 43
Palazzo dei Normanni (Palace of the Normans) 43
Quattro Canti (Four Corners) 46
Teatro Massimo 48
Norman Cathedral of Palermo 50
Catacombe dei Cappuccini (Capuchin Catacombs) 52
Zisa Palace 54
La Cuba 56
Vucciria Market 58
Fontana Pretoria (Pretoria Fountain) 61
Castello di Cefalà Diana 64
Villa palagonia 67
MUSEUMS AND ART GALLERIES 70
Palazzo dei Normanni Museum 70
Museo Archeologico Regionale 72
Museo Internazionale delle Marionette Antonio Pasqualino 74
Museo delle Maioliche Stanze al Genio 76
Cantieri Culturali alla Zisa 78
Etnografico Siciliano Museum 80
Palazzo Abatellis 82
Modern Art at GAM Palermo 84
CATHEDRALS AND RELIGIOUS SITES 87

Cattedrale di Palermo 87
Cappella Palatina 90
San Giovanni degli Eremiti 92
Oratorio di San Lorenzo 94
Santuario Santa Rosalia 96
La Martorana 98
The Palatine Chapel 100
Church of Saint John of the Hermits 102
STATUES AND MONUMENTS 105
Statue of Carlo V 106
Statue of Ruggero Settimo 108
Statue of Giuseppe Garibaldi 111
Statue of the Genius of Palermo (Il Genio di Palermo) 113
Statue of Santa Rosalia 115
Statue of Vincenzo Florio 118
Giuseppe verdi statue 120
Statue of Saint Francis of Paola 123
Bronze bust of Bernardino da Ucria 125
CULTURAL TREASURES 127
The Opera 127
Baroque Architecture 129
Arab-Norman Architecture 132
Artistic Expressions 134

NATURE ADVENTURES 137
Mountain Hikes in Palermo 137
Beaches and Coastal Beauty in Palermo 139
Gardens and Oases in Palermo 141
Nature Reserves in Palermo 143
National Parks in Palermo 144
Wildlife in Palermo 146
BEST ACTIVITIES 148
Mountain Biking in the Madonie Mountains 149
Hiking in the Zingaro Nature Reserve 149
Rock Climbing at Monte Pellegrino 150
Kayaking along Sicily's Coastline 150
Snorkeling and Diving in Isola delle Femmine 150
Countryside Horseback Riding 150
Sailing in the Tyrrhenian Sea 151
Camping under the Sicilian Sky 151
Water activities 152
Breathtaking Sunset spots 157
LOCAL FOOD MARKETS AND STREET LIFE 160
Vibrant Markets 161
Street Food 163
Ballarò Market 166
Capo Market 168

PALERMO TOURS 171
Historical Walking Tour 171
Street Food Tour 174
Art and Architecture Tour 176
Nighttime Ghost Tour 178
Palermo Bike Tour 181
Segway Tour 183
Mafia History Tour 186
Wine Tasting Tour 189
Cooking Class and Market Tour 191
DAY TRIPS 194
Cefalù 195
Monreale 197
Agrigento 199
Segesta 201
Erice 203
Trapani 205
Selinunte 207
Marsala 209
Egadi Islands 211
ITINERARIES 214
Historical Marvels and Cultural Immersion 214
Artistic Treasures and Culinary Delights 215

Architecture and Ancient Sites 215
Palermo by Night 216
Gardens and Relaxation 216
Religious Heritage and Spiritual Exploration 216
Architecture and Modern Art 217
Palermo's Seaside Charm 217
Market Exploration and Local Flavors 218
Palermo's Hidden Gems 218
MAPS 220
City Map 220
Teatro Massimo Map 221
Palermo Cathedral 222
Accommodation Map 223
Parks and Green Spaces Map 224
CONCLUSION 225
INDEX 226

INTRODUCTION

Welcome to Palermo, the vibrant and captivating cultural hub of Sicily. As we step into Palermo in 2023 and beyond, we invite you to immerse yourself in a world where history, architecture, art, and cuisine merge to create a tapestry of unique experiences. Palermo is a city where layers of civilizations have left their mark, resulting in a destination that is as diverse as it is captivating.

Palermo beckons travelers to explore its narrow alleys, grand palaces, and bustling markets. From the Byzantine mosaics of the Palatine Chapel to the aroma of freshly baked sfincione in the air, this city tells the story of Sicily's rich past and its vibrant present. Whether you're wandering through its historic streets, savoring local delicacies, or admiring its architectural wonders, Palermo promises a journey that will awaken your senses and ignite your curiosity.

In this travel guide, we will delve into the heart of Palermo, uncovering its hidden gems, embracing its cultural diversity, and celebrating the warmth of its people. From the impressive Cattedrale di Palermo to the lively street markets that come alive with colors and aromas, Palermo invites you to experience the essence of Sicily in all its splendor.

IMPORTANT INFORMATION

Embarking on a journey to Palermo is an exciting endeavor, and being well-prepared ensures a smooth and enjoyable experience. Here are some essential travel details to keep in mind as you plan your trip:

Basic Information

Passport and Visa Requirements:

Ensure your passport is valid for at least six months beyond your intended departure date. Depending on your nationality, you might require a visa to enter Italy. Check with the Italian embassy or consulate in your country for the most up-to-date information.

Health and Insurance:

Consider obtaining travel insurance that covers medical emergencies, trip cancellations, and lost belongings. It's also a good idea to have a copy of your health insurance details, any necessary vaccinations, and any prescription medications you may need during your trip.

Currency and Banking:

The currency used in Italy is the Euro (EUR). ATMs are widely available throughout Palermo, and credit cards are generally accepted in most establishments. Notify your bank of your travel dates to avoid any issues with using your cards abroad.

Language:

The official language in Italy is Italian. While English is commonly spoken in tourist areas, having a basic understanding of Italian phrases can be helpful for communication.

Weather and Clothing:

Palermo enjoys a Mediterranean climate, with mild winters and hot summers. Pack accordingly with lightweight clothing for the summer months and some warmer layers for the evenings and cooler months.

Local Customs and Etiquette:

It's customary to greet with a handshake and maintain eye contact while conversing. When visiting churches or religious sites, dress modestly by covering your shoulders and wearing knee-length clothing.

Transportation:

Palermo has an efficient public transportation system, including buses and trams. Taxis and rideshare services are also available. Consider purchasing a Palermo Card for discounted transportation and attraction entry.

Safety and Emergency Contacts:

Palermo is generally safe for travelers, but it's wise to exercise the same caution you would in any major city. Keep a photocopy of important documents in a separate location, and note down local emergency numbers.

Local Cuisine:

Indulge in Sicilian cuisine by trying local specialties such as arancini, panelle, and pasta con le sarde. Sicily is also known for its delicious gelato and pastries.

Cultural Sensitivity:

Respect local customs and traditions, especially when visiting religious sites. Keep in mind that different cultures may have different norms regarding public behavior.

Stay Informed:

Stay updated with the latest travel advisories and health guidelines, especially in light of any global events. Monitor the news and information from official sources before and during your trip.

Port of Palermo

The Port of Palermo, also known as "Porto di Palermo" in Italian, is a major seaport located in Palermo, the capital city of Sicily, Italy. It is one of the largest and busiest ports in the Mediterranean Sea, serving as a vital transportation and commercial hub for the region. Here are some key details about the Port of Palermo:

Location:

The Port of Palermo is strategically situated on the northern coast of Sicily, along the Tyrrhenian Sea. Its location makes it an important gateway for maritime trade and transportation between Sicily, mainland Italy, and other Mediterranean countries.

Historical Significance:

The port has a rich maritime history that dates back centuries. It has played a significant role in the commercial and cultural exchange between Sicily and various Mediterranean civilizations, including Phoenicians, Romans, Arabs, and Normans.

Commercial Activities:

The Port of Palermo is a vital center for trade and commerce. It handles a wide range of cargo, including containers, bulk goods, and general cargo. It also serves as a hub for the distribution of goods to and from the Sicilian region.

Passenger Services:

In addition to its cargo operations, the port provides passenger services. It serves as a departure and arrival point for both domestic and international ferry routes, connecting Sicily to the Italian mainland and neighboring Mediterranean islands.

Tourism:

The port area has undergone development and beautification in recent years, making it a more attractive destination for tourists. Visitors can enjoy the waterfront promenade, various restaurants, and cultural attractions near the port.

Marina and Yachting:

The Port of Palermo has a marina known as "Cala," which caters to recreational boating and yachting. It offers facilities and services for boaters and tourists exploring the city by sea.

Cruise Ship Terminal:

Palermo is a popular cruise ship destination, and the port features a dedicated cruise ship terminal. It welcomes cruise ships from around the world, bringing tourists to explore Palermo and its surrounding areas.

Transportation Hub:

The port's proximity to the city center makes it an important transportation hub for both goods and passengers. It is well-connected to the city's road and rail networks, facilitating the movement of cargo and travelers.

Development and Modernization:

Over the years, the Port of Palermo has undergone modernization and expansion efforts to meet the demands of international trade and tourism while preserving its historical significance.

Accommodation in Palermo

Finding the perfect accommodation for your journey to Palermo is a crucial aspect of ensuring a comfortable and enjoyable stay. Here is a carefully curated list of recommended accommodations, each offering a unique experience that complements the city's charm and character.

Grand Hotel Piazza Borsa

Situated in the heart of Palermo, the Grand Hotel Piazza Borsa seamlessly blends historical elegance with modern luxury. The hotel is housed within a beautifully restored 16th-century building and offers spacious rooms, a spa, and a rooftop terrace overlooking the city. Its central location allows easy access to major attractions and the bustling markets.

Hotel Principe di Villafranca

This boutique hotel exudes contemporary sophistication while preserving its historical architecture. The Hotel Principe di Villafranca boasts stylishly designed rooms, a charming courtyard, and a bar that serves both classic and innovative cocktails. The hotel's location in the city center provides a convenient base for exploring Palermo's cultural gems.

Grand Hotel Wagner

For a taste of old-world opulence, the Grand Hotel Wagner is a prime choice. Named after the famous composer Richard Wagner, this hotel radiates an elegant ambiance with its period furnishings and classic décor. The hotel's proximity to the Teatro Massimo and other landmarks adds to its appeal.

Massimo Plaza Hotel

Situated just steps away from the iconic Teatro Massimo, the Massimo Plaza Hotel offers modern comforts in a prime location. The hotel's rooms are tastefully decorated and equipped with modern amenities. The rooftop terrace provides a panoramic view of Palermo's skyline, making it an ideal spot to unwind.

Casa Nostra Luxury Suites

For a more intimate experience, consider Casa Nostra Luxury Suites. This boutique guesthouse offers elegantly designed suites with a mix of contemporary and vintage elements. The personalized service and attention to detail create a home-away-from-home atmosphere.

B&B Palermo Art

If you're seeking a cozy bed and breakfast experience, B&B Palermo Art is a delightful choice. The owner's passion for art is evident in every corner, with each room adorned with unique artwork. The central location and warm hospitality make for a memorable stay.

Palazzo Natoli Boutique Hotel

Experience Palermo's history firsthand by staying in a beautifully restored palazzo. The Palazzo Natoli Boutique Hotel offers elegantly appointed rooms that blend modern comfort with historical charm. The attentive staff and central location contribute to an unforgettable stay.

FAQ

As you prepare for your journey to Palermo, it's natural to have questions about the city, its attractions, logistics, and more. Here are answers to some commonly asked questions to help you make the most of your Palermo adventure:

What are the must-visit attractions in Palermo?

Palermo is brimming with attractions. Don't miss the Palazzo dei Normanni, the Cappella Palatina, Quattro Canti, Teatro Massimo, and the vibrant markets like Ballarò and Vucciria.

What is the best time to visit Palermo?

Spring (April to June) and fall (September to October) are ideal for pleasant weather and fewer crowds. Summers can be hot and busy, while winters are mild with occasional rain.

How do I get around Palermo?

Palermo has a well-connected public transportation system comprising buses and trams. Taxis and rideshare services are also readily available. Walking is a great way to explore the city's historic center.

Is English widely spoken in Palermo?

While Italian is the official language, English is commonly spoken in tourist areas, hotels, and restaurants. Having a few basic Italian phrases can enhance your experience.

What is the local cuisine like in Palermo?

Palermo's cuisine is a fusion of Italian, Arab, and Mediterranean influences. Try arancini (rice balls), pasta con le sarde (pasta with sardines), panelle (chickpea fritters), and sample the array of fresh seafood.

Are credit cards widely accepted in Palermo?

Yes, credit cards are generally accepted in most establishments, especially in tourist areas. However, it's a good idea to have some cash on hand for smaller shops and markets.

Are there any cultural customs I should be aware of?

Italians value politeness and greeting with a handshake is common. When visiting churches, dress modestly by covering your shoulders and wearing knee-length clothing.

What are some hidden gems to explore in Palermo?

Venture beyond the main attractions to discover hidden gems like the Oratorio di San Lorenzo, Mercato del Capo, and the Kalsa neighborhood for a more local experience.

Are there any COVID-19 travel restrictions or guidelines in place?

Travel regulations can change due to the evolving pandemic situation. Stay updated with the latest travel advisories, entry requirements, and health guidelines from official sources before your trip.

How can I experience Palermo's cultural scene?

Explore art galleries, attend music and theater festivals, and participate in local events to immerse yourself in Palermo's vibrant cultural scene.

PALERMO HISTORY

Nestled on the northern coast of Sicily, Palermo stands as a living testament to the ebb and flow of centuries, where cultures, civilizations, and dynasties have converged to shape the city's rich history. From its ancient origins to its contemporary vibrancy, Palermo's historical narrative is a captivating tale that continues to unfold.

Ancient Roots and Early Settlers

The story of Palermo's origins is a voyage through antiquity, where the earliest settlers and civilizations laid the foundation for a city that would flourish over millennia. As we delve into the ancient roots of Palermo, we uncover the captivating narrative that began with the first footsteps upon its shores.

Phoenician Pioneers

Around 734 BC, the Phoenicians, renowned seafarers and traders, cast their gaze upon the northern coast of Sicily and recognized its strategic potential. Palermo, nestled between hills and the azure Mediterranean, was selected as the site for a Phoenician trading post. These pioneers established a connection to the sea that would shape Palermo's identity for centuries to come.

A Trading Hub Emerges

The Phoenicians were soon joined by other ancient civilizations, each leaving an imprint on the burgeoning settlement. The Carthaginians, successors to the Phoenicians, recognized Palermo's economic significance and bolstered its status as a maritime trading hub. With its natural harbor and access to regional resources, Palermo thrived as a center of commerce, attracting traders from distant lands.

Roman Rule and Urban Evolution

In 254 BC, the Romans conquered Palermo and integrated it into their expanding empire. The city, now known as Panormus, underwent urban development, witnessing the construction of temples, forums, and amphitheaters. Roman influence transformed the landscape, laying the groundwork for Palermo's transformation from a trading outpost to a bustling urban center.

A Tapestry of Cultures

As centuries passed, Palermo's allure drew the attention of successive civilizations. The Vandals, Ostrogoths, and Byzantines each left their mark, adding layers to the city's cultural tapestry. The Byzantine era, in particular, introduced new architectural styles and religious influences, reflected in the city's ecclesiastical structures and mosaics.

A Glimpse of the Past

The echoes of these ancient settlers still resonate in Palermo's streets, architecture, and cultural heritage. The Phoenician foundation, the Carthaginian spirit of trade, the Roman penchant for urban planning, and the Byzantine touch of artistry all converge to create a unique identity that defines Palermo.

Byzantine and Arab Influences

In the annals of Palermo's history, the eras of Byzantine and Arab influences stand as chapters that have profoundly shaped the city's identity. These periods, marked by artistic brilliance, intellectual enlightenment, and cultural exchange, have left an indelible imprint on Palermo's architecture, traditions, and way of life.

Byzantine Artistry and Spiritual Flourish

As the Byzantine Empire extended its dominion over Palermo in the 6th century, a wave of transformation swept through the city. Ecclesiastical architecture flourished, adorned with intricate mosaics and ornate frescoes. The religious fervor of this era manifested in iconic structures like the Church of San Giovanni degli Eremiti, characterized by its red domes, reflecting Byzantine architectural influences.

Arab Magnificence and Urban Elegance

The 9th century ushered in a new epoch as the Arab conquest brought Palermo under Islamic rule. This period marked a zenith of cultural exchange, enlightenment, and architectural innovation. The Arab rulers embraced the city, fostering an atmosphere of intellectual curiosity and artistic expression. Palermo became a beacon of learning, with libraries and schools that attracted scholars from across the Mediterranean. The Arab influence is perhaps most pronounced in Palermo's architecture. Elaborate arches, intricate stucco work, and vibrant ceramics became hallmarks of the Arab style. The most iconic embodiment of this influence is the Zisa, a summer palace characterized by its geometric patterns, fountains, and lush gardens.

Cultural Fusion and Architectural Legacy

The confluence of Byzantine and Arab influences engendered a unique cultural fusion that is Palermo's hallmark. The city's architecture became a canvas on which these two worlds intertwined, producing masterpieces like the Palazzo dei Normanni and the Cappella Palatina. The latter, a chapel within the palace, is a testament to the harmony achieved through the blending of Norman, Byzantine, and Arab artistic elements.

Legacy of Cosmopolitan Harmony

The legacy of Byzantine and Arab influences endures in Palermo's vibrant culture and architectural heritage. Streets lined with palm trees, domes adorned with intricate mosaics, and flavors infused with Middle Eastern spices evoke a sense of timelessness that resonates with the city's multicultural past.

Norman Conquest and Cultural Fusion

The Norman conquest of Palermo in the 11th century marked a pivotal juncture in the city's history, one that catalyzed a remarkable period of cultural fusion, architectural splendor, and cross-cultural exchange. This era of convergence between Norman, Byzantine, Arab, and indigenous influences not only transformed Palermo's physical landscape but also left an enduring legacy that resonates to this day.

The Norman Arrival and an Era of Change

In 1072, the Normans, under the leadership of Robert Guiscard, captured Palermo, ushering in a new era of governance and cultural interplay. The Normans, renowned for their affinity for adopting and adapting to local traditions, embraced the multicultural character of the city. This acceptance laid the groundwork for a unique and harmonious coexistence of diverse cultures.

Architectural Marvels: A Synthesis of Styles

The Norman rulers initiated a construction boom that blended Norman, Byzantine, and Arab architectural elements. The Palazzo dei Normanni, the grand Norman palace, stands as a testament to this fusion, with its intricate mosaics, Byzantine-influenced dome, and Arab-inspired arches. The Cappella Palatina, nested within the palace, exemplifies this architectural amalgamation, where Norman, Arab, and Byzantine artistic styles interlace seamlessly.

The Cappella Palatina: A Microcosm of Harmony

Perhaps the most resplendent representation of the Norman conquest's impact is the Cappella Palatina. This small chapel encapsulates the essence of cultural fusion, featuring Byzantine mosaics that narrate biblical stories, Arab-inspired stucco decoration, and Norman architectural forms. Within its walls, a harmonious symphony of artistic expressions from different civilizations resounds, symbolizing the unity achieved amidst diversity.

A Cultural Renaissance Unveiled

The Norman period not only flourished architecturally but also fostered intellectual and artistic renaissance. The translation of Arabic texts into Latin opened doors to a wealth of knowledge, spurring innovation in medicine, science, and philosophy. The city's vibrant markets became hubs of cultural exchange, as commodities and ideas flowed freely among diverse communities.

Legacy and Contemporary Reflections

The cultural synthesis achieved during the Norman era endures as a cornerstone of Palermo's identity. Contemporary Palermo continues to honor this legacy, with its multicultural spirit manifested in art, cuisine, and daily life. The embrace of diversity remains a poignant reminder of the power of unity through differences.

Spanish Domination and Baroque Splendor

The chapter of Spanish domination in Palermo's history unfolded against a backdrop of opulence, artistic innovation, and architectural grandeur. This era, spanning the 16th to 18th centuries, witnessed the flourishing of Baroque art and culture, leaving an indelible mark on the city's skyline and identity.

Spanish Rule and Cultural Influence

The Spanish conquest of Palermo in 1516 marked the city's integration into the Spanish Empire. During this period, Palermo's strategic significance as a Mediterranean port flourished, igniting an era of economic growth and cultural exchange. The Spanish rulers, much like their predecessors, embraced the city's multicultural heritage and contributed to the vibrant fusion of traditions.

Baroque Aesthetics: Ornate Extravagance

The Baroque period, characterized by its exuberant and elaborate artistic style, found its way to Palermo through the hands of Spanish architects, sculptors, and painters. The city's architecture underwent a transformation marked by grandeur, theatricality, and intricate details. Facades were adorned with sculptures, frescoes, and ornate stucco work, creating a visual symphony that captivated the senses.

Quattro Canti: The Intersection of Grandeur

At the heart of Palermo, the Quattro Canti (Four Corners) intersection became a quintessential example of the Baroque aesthetic. This octagonal crossroads features four ornate facades, each representing a season, a Spanish king, and a patron saint. The Quattro Canti is a living testament to the city's commitment to expressing its grandeur through architectural mastery.

Churches as Artistic Masterpieces

Religious fervor also found its expression in the Baroque era, with churches becoming canvases for artistic brilliance. The Chiesa di Santa Caterina, for example, dazzles with its intricate decorations, while the Chiesa del Gesù showcases elaborate altars and gilded details that transport visitors into a world of spiritual awe and artistic splendor.

Continued Influence and Modern Reflections

Palermo's Baroque legacy continues to influence the city's aesthetic and cultural landscape. The ornate architecture, artistic fervor, and attention to detail remain integral to Palermo's identity. The Baroque period's legacy extends beyond the physical structures, shaping the city's ethos of embracing the grandeur of life.

Unification of Italy and Modernization

The 19th century brought a wave of transformation to Palermo, as the city became intricately woven into the fabric of Italy's unification. This period of change, marked by social upheaval and modernization efforts, shaped Palermo's trajectory and set the stage for its role in the modern era.

Unification and Sociopolitical Shifts

The mid-19th century witnessed the unification of Italy, a pivotal event that united diverse regions under a single national identity. Palermo, as a vital center of commerce and culture, played a significant role in this process. The city's population engaged in fervent discussions on political ideologies, and its streets saw both celebration and turmoil as the unification movement gained momentum.

Modernization and Urban Transformation

With the unification of Italy came aspirations for modernization, and Palermo was no exception. The city underwent ambitious urban planning projects that aimed to revamp its infrastructure and improve the quality of life for its inhabitants. Roads were widened, public buildings were erected, and transportation systems were developed, transforming Palermo's urban landscape.

Preserving the Past Amidst Progress

While modernization brought many benefits, it also raised concerns about preserving Palermo's rich historical heritage. Efforts were made to strike a balance between embracing progress and safeguarding the city's architectural treasures. This delicate equilibrium between the old and the new remains a defining aspect of Palermo's character.

Cultural Resilience and Contemporary Impact

The challenges of the 19th century did not extinguish Palermo's cultural spirit. The city continued to be a hub of artistic and intellectual activity, with theaters, academies, and cultural institutions flourishing. Palermo's role as a cultural center continued to evolve, reflecting the city's capacity to adapt to changing times.

Modern Palermo: A Dynamic Fusion

As the 20th century unfolded, Palermo continued to navigate the currents of modernity while honoring its past. The city's ability to blend tradition with progress remains evident in its architecture, cuisine, and way of life. Palermo's vibrant street markets, historic neighborhoods, and modern cultural events stand as a testament to its dynamic fusion of old and new.

Contemporary Palermo

Stepping into contemporary Palermo is embarking on a journey that encapsulates the city's ability to blend history with innovation, tradition with modernity, and cultural diversity with a shared sense of identity. As we explore Palermo in the present day, we find a city that embraces its past while looking towards a future of sustainability, creativity, and continued transformation.

Cultural Renaissance and Artistic Expression

Palermo's contemporary landscape is marked by a thriving cultural renaissance. The city's vibrant arts scene has expanded to encompass modern galleries, music festivals, and creative spaces. International artists are drawn to Palermo's rich history and diverse influences, resulting in a dynamic fusion of global perspectives and local traditions.

Hidden Gems and Neighborhood Revitalization

While iconic sites remain essential, contemporary Palermo invites exploration beyond the well-trodden paths. Neighborhoods that were once considered "off the beaten track" are now blossoming with cultural hubs, boutique shops, and innovative eateries. These hidden gems showcase a different side of Palermo, one that reflects its evolution and diversity.

Culinary Evolution and Fusion

Palermo's culinary scene has evolved, embracing modern trends while holding steadfast to its traditional roots. A new generation of chefs and food artisans experiment with innovative ingredients and techniques, reinterpreting classic dishes while maintaining the essence of Sicilian cuisine. The result is a gastronomic landscape that mirrors the city's dynamic spirit.

Cultural Festivals and Global Exchange

Palermo's contemporary identity is also shaped by its participation in global cultural exchange. Festivals celebrating cinema, music, and literature draw artists and enthusiasts from around the world, fostering cross-cultural dialogue and reinforcing Palermo's place as a cosmopolitan city.

HISTORIC DISTRICTS

Palermo's historic districts are like chapters in a captivating novel, each one unfolding a story that spans centuries of culture, architecture, and human interaction. As you traverse these enchanting districts in 2023 and beyond, you'll be transported through time, witnessing the evolution of Palermo from its ancient roots to the modern era. Join us as we unveil the tapestry of history woven into the very fabric of the city.

La Kalsa

In the heart of Palermo lies the captivating district of La Kalsa, a living testament to the city's rich and diverse history. In the year 2023 and beyond, as you step into the cobblestone streets of La Kalsa, you'll find yourself transported through time, immersed in a world where Arab influences, historic architecture, and contemporary life intertwine to create a tapestry of culture and identity.

A Glimpse into the Past

La Kalsa, derived from the Arabic word "al-Khalisa," meaning "the chosen," encapsulates the Arab legacy that once shaped the city. The district's winding streets, narrow alleys, and architecture echo the intricate urban planning of the Arab settlers who left an indelible mark on Palermo.

Arab Influence and Architecture

The Arab influence is evident in the architectural details of La Kalsa, where horseshoe arches, intricate stucco work, and decorative motifs recall the aesthetics of the past. As you stroll through the district, you'll encounter historic buildings that showcase a harmonious blend of Norman, Byzantine, and Arab styles—a testament to the multicultural heritage of Palermo.

Piazzas and Hidden Gems

La Kalsa is adorned with charming piazzas that invite you to pause and absorb the atmosphere. Piazza Kalsa, with its elegant palaces and churches, transports you to another era, while Piazza Marina offers a serene escape surrounded by greenery and historic landmarks. As you explore the district, you'll also uncover hidden gems, such as the Oratorio dei Bianchi with its exquisite frescoes.

Contemporary Vibrancy

La Kalsa isn't just a relic of the past; it's a district where history converges with modern life. As you walk along its streets, you'll encounter artisan workshops, galleries, and cafes that infuse a contemporary vibrancy into the historical backdrop. This blend of old and new reflects Palermo's ability to evolve while preserving its cultural roots.

Cultural Fusion and Identity

La Kalsa is more than just a physical district; it's a manifestation of Palermo's identity. The district's past as a melting pot of cultures and religions is a reminder of the city's open-mindedness and adaptability—a legacy that continues to shape its present and future.

Albergheria

Nestled within the heart of Palermo, the district of Albergheria beckons you to embark on a journey through time. In the year 2023 and beyond, as you wander through its labyrinthine streets, you'll find yourself transported to an era where medieval charm coexists with the vibrancy of contemporary life. Albergheria is a district that encapsulates Palermo's multifaceted identity, where historic landmarks, bustling markets, and the pulse of modernity converge.

Medieval Grandeur and Architectural Heritage

Albergheria is a district steeped in history, where grandeur and architectural diversity tell the story of Palermo's evolution. The imposing Cattedrale di Palermo, with its Norman towers and Gothic spires, stands as a sentinel of the city's past. Nearby, the breathtaking Cappella Palatina showcases the intricate beauty of Byzantine artistry, transporting you to a time when cultures converged to create something truly remarkable.

Bustling Markets and Authentic Palermo

Venture into Albergheria's streets and you'll encounter vibrant markets that offer a sensory feast. Vucciria Market, with its colorful stalls and lively atmosphere, harks back to Palermo's bustling street life. Capo Market, with its array of fresh produce, seafood, and local delicacies, immerses you in the authentic flavors of Sicilian cuisine. These markets are not just places to shop; they're windows into the city's culinary and cultural soul.

Historic Piazzas and Urban Exploration

The district's historic piazzas are gathering points where locals and visitors converge. Piazza Pretoria, with its stunning fountain and ornate architecture, invites contemplation. Piazza Bellini, surrounded by churches and palaces, exudes a sense of timeless elegance. Exploring the district's alleyways and hidden corners is a rewarding adventure, as each turn reveals another facet of Palermo's rich heritage.

Palermo's Aristocratic Past and Modern Resilience

Albergheria showcases the city's aristocratic heritage through its palatial residences and grand squares. The district around the Palazzo dei Normanni is a living reminder of Palermo's noble history. As you walk through Albergheria's streets, you'll also encounter contemporary cafes, boutiques, and galleries that reflect the district's ability to adapt and evolve while preserving its historical charm.

Cultural Tapestry and Identity

Albergheria isn't just a district; it's a microcosm of Palermo's identity. The convergence of architectural styles, the juxtaposition of historic and modern elements, and the blend of cultural influences reflect the city's mosaic-like character. As you navigate its streets, you're traversing the threads that weave together Palermo's past, present, and future.

Vucciria

In the heart of Palermo, the district of Vucciria unfolds as a vibrant canvas of colors, aromas, and lively street scenes. As you step into its bustling alleys in 2023 and beyond, you'll find yourself immersed in the authentic essence of Palermo's street life—an experience that connects you with the city's rich history, its culinary traditions, and the vibrant spirit of its people.

A Burst of Energy

Vucciria is more than just a district; it's a living spectacle that pulsates with energy. The name "Vucciria" itself derives from the Sicilian word "bucceria," meaning "confusion," which perfectly encapsulates the lively and chaotic atmosphere of the area. As you navigate its narrow streets, you'll be greeted by a kaleidoscope of colors, the shouts of vendors, and the chatter of locals—a sensory feast that's both invigorating and exhilarating.

Historic Roots and Artistic Inspiration

Vucciria has been a bustling market for centuries, dating back to the Arab rule of Palermo. This history is evident in the district's street layout, its architectural elements, and its enduring commitment to commerce and trade. The district's vibrant ambiance has also been a source of inspiration for artists, writers, and filmmakers, capturing the dynamic essence of Palermo's urban life.

Culinary Delights and Street Food

One of the highlights of Vucciria is its culinary offerings. Street food stalls offer a mouthwatering array of Palermo's iconic delicacies. Indulge in the savory delights of panelle (chickpea fritters) and arancine (stuffed rice balls). Let the aroma of freshly grilled salsiccia (sausage) and the sweet allure of cannoli guide your senses toward unforgettable flavors that are deeply rooted in Sicilian tradition.

Artisan Shops and Authentic Finds

Beyond the lively food scene, Vucciria is a treasure trove of artisan shops and traditional crafts. As you explore the district, you'll encounter local artisans who proudly showcase their handmade goods—be it intricate ceramics, leather goods, or souvenirs that capture the essence of Palermo's artistic heritage.

Cultural Immersion and Local Connection

Vucciria isn't just a place to visit; it's an invitation to immerse yourself in Palermo's local culture. Engage in conversations with vendors, haggle over prices, and allow yourself to become a part of the dynamic street life. These interactions provide insights into the warmth and hospitality that define Palermo's identity.

Capo

In the heart of Palermo lies a district that invites you to uncover the city's soul through its vibrant markets—Capo. As you traverse its bustling streets in 2023 and beyond, you'll step into a world of sensory delights, where the aromas, colors, and sounds of local life merge to create an authentic experience that immerses you in Palermo's cultural tapestry.

A Feast for the Senses

Capo is a district where every sense is engaged. The air is filled with the fragrance of fresh produce, the sizzle of grilling meats, and the tantalizing scent of spices. The vivid colors of fruits, vegetables, and seafood create a visual symphony that's both captivating and inspiring. As you navigate the bustling markets, you'll feel the rhythm of Palermo's daily life—the pulse of a city that's deeply rooted in its culinary traditions.

Palermo's Culinary Essence

The markets of Capo are more than just places to shop; they're windows into Palermo's gastronomic identity. Here, you'll find an array of local ingredients that are the building blocks of Sicilian cuisine. From the rich flavors of olive oil and the allure of sun-ripened tomatoes to the succulent seafood that's a cornerstone of coastal life, the markets of Capo are a celebration of the region's culinary bounty.

Local Flavors and Traditions

Indulge in the diverse array of street food that Capo offers. Sink your teeth into the savory delight of panelle and the crispy goodness of crocchè. Savor the distinctive taste of panelle e crocchè sandwiches—a local favorite that's both comforting and satisfying. These flavors are more than just food; they're a direct link to Palermo's history and cultural heritage.

Hidden Treasures and Authentic Interactions

Capo is a district that thrives on the authenticity of its interactions. Engage with the local vendors, strike up conversations, and allow yourself to be swept up in the lively atmosphere. Whether you're bargaining for the freshest catch of the day or sampling a slice of cassata from a pastry shop, you're not just engaging with the products; you're connecting with the people who have dedicated their lives to their craft.

A Cultural Symphony

Capo is more than just a marketplace; it's a cultural symphony that harmonizes the past and present. The markets' historic roots and contemporary vibrancy create an experience that's both timeless and dynamic. As you immerse yourself in the district's ambiance, you're connecting with a centuries-old tradition of trade, commerce, and the shared experience of the Palermitans.

Kalsa-Marina

Along the waterfront of Palermo, the district of Kalsa-Marina stands as a testament to the city's timeless allure and its deep connection with the sea. As you explore its charming streets in 2023 and beyond, you'll be enveloped in an atmosphere of elegance, history, and natural beauty—a symphony that unites Palermo's aristocratic past with its vibrant present.

Seaside Elegance and Architectural Splendor

Kalsa-Marina is a district that exudes an air of sophistication. The grandeur of historic palaces, churches, and noble residences reflects the district's aristocratic past. As you walk along its streets, you'll encounter architectural marvels that pay homage to Palermo's noble heritage, each façade telling a story of a bygone era.

Stunning Seascapes and Coastal Charm

One of the defining features of Kalsa-Marina is its breathtaking seafront. The district's proximity to the Mediterranean Sea offers unparalleled vistas that invite contemplation. Whether you're watching the sun set over the waves, taking a leisurely stroll along the promenade, or enjoying a meal at a seaside restaurant, you'll be captivated by the ever-present allure of the sea.

Cultural Crossroads and Multicultural History

Kalsa-Marina is a district that embodies Palermo's history as a cultural crossroads. The influence of various civilizations is evident in its architecture and atmosphere. Norman, Arab, and Spanish influences converge to create a unique blend that's both harmonious and intriguing. This district reflects Palermo's ability to embrace diversity and create something truly special.

Piazzas of Elegance and Tranquility

The piazzas of Kalsa-Marina are like tranquil oases where you can pause and soak in the district's ambiance. Piazza Marina, with its lush greenery and historic palaces, offers a serene escape from the bustle of the city. Piazza Magione, adorned with a historic church, exudes an air of quiet elegance that invites reflection.

Modern Flourish and Cultural Evolution

While steeped in history, Kalsa-Marina isn't frozen in time. Contemporary cafes, boutiques, and galleries seamlessly blend with the district's historic charm. This juxtaposition of old and new reflects Palermo's ability to evolve while maintaining its cultural roots.

Palazzo dei Normanni District

In the heart of Palermo, the district surrounding the Palazzo dei Normanni beckons you to step into a world of aristocratic grandeur, historical significance, and cultural depth. As you explore its elegant streets in 2023 and beyond, you'll find yourself immersed in a journey through time—a journey that unveils Palermo's noble past and its enduring influence on the city's identity.

Aristocratic Splendor and Cultural Heritage

The district surrounding the Palazzo dei Normanni is a living testament to Palermo's aristocratic history. The palazzo itself, also known as the Royal Palace, has stood for centuries as a symbol of power and authority. Its imposing presence, adorned with architectural details and historical significance, invites you to delve into the lives of those who once walked its halls.

Cappella Palatina: A Jewel of Multicultural Artistry

Within the Palazzo dei Normanni lies the Cappella Palatina, a masterpiece that transcends cultural boundaries. As you step into this exquisite chapel, you'll be enveloped in a world where Norman, Byzantine, and Arab influences converge. The intricate mosaics, the ornate wooden ceiling, and the harmonious blend of artistic styles create an environment that's both spiritually inspiring and culturally enlightening.

Architectural Diversity and Timeless Elegance

The district's architectural diversity is a testament to Palermo's ability to adapt and evolve. As you explore its streets, you'll encounter a blend of styles that tell the story of different epochs. From the Norman-Arab architecture of the

Zisa Palace to the elegant facades of noble residences, each structure reflects a chapter in Palermo's history.

Piazza Indipendenza: Echoes of Modernity

Piazza Indipendenza, located near the Palazzo dei Normanni, serves as a nod to modernity while maintaining a connection with the past. This bustling square is surrounded by historic buildings, such as the Palazzo d'Orleans, and offers a glimpse into contemporary life while remaining rooted in the district's heritage.

Cultural Nexus and Identity

The Palazzo dei Normanni District is more than just a collection of buildings; it's a cultural nexus that defines Palermo's identity. It encapsulates the city's ability to embrace diversity, honor its past, and create a harmonious blend of historical significance and contemporary vibrancy.

La Loggia District

Nestled within the heart of Palermo, the La Loggia district unfolds as a hidden gem that invites you to explore its charm and uncover the layers of history woven into its streets. In 2023 and beyond, as you venture into this district, you'll find yourself immersed in a world where architectural splendor, artistic creativity, and a sense of community converge to create an experience that's both enriching and delightful.

Architectural Marvels and Renaissance Flair

La Loggia is known for its architectural marvels that exude a sense of elegance and refinement. The district is named after the Loggia dei Pisani—a stunning example of Renaissance architecture. Its graceful arches, ornate details, and harmonious proportions showcase Palermo's connection with the artistic trends of the past.

Artistic Expressions and Creativity

The district of La Loggia is a haven for artists and creative minds. As you explore its streets, you'll encounter galleries, studios, and artisan workshops that breathe life into the district's artistic spirit. The vibrant community of creators contributes to the district's unique ambiance and its role as a hub of creative expression.

Historic Streets and Hidden Corners

La Loggia invites you to wander through its historic streets and discover hidden corners that tell stories of generations past. Cobblestone pathways, quaint squares, and charming facades create an atmosphere that's both evocative and picturesque. Each turn offers a new perspective, inviting you to take your time and immerse yourself in the district's ambiance.

Local Culture and Community Connection

La Loggia isn't just a district; it's a community where locals gather, share stories, and celebrate their identity. The district's cafes, taverns, and piazzas serve as meeting points where you can engage with the warmth and hospitality of the Palermitans. These interactions provide insights into the genuine connections that define the district's character.

Timelessness and Modern Evolution

La Loggia is a district where time seems to stand still, yet it's also a place where modernity flourishes. While embracing its historic roots, the district seamlessly integrates contemporary elements that reflect Palermo's ability to evolve while preserving its heritage.

HISTORICAL SITES AND LANDMARKS

Palermo is a treasure trove of historical sites that bear witness to the city's diverse heritage and rich tapestry of civilizations. As you embark on a journey to uncover Palermo's past, these historical sites stand as monuments to centuries of culture, art, and architectural innovation.

Palazzo dei Normanni (Palace of the Normans)

Nestled in the heart of Palermo, the Palazzo dei Normanni stands as a resplendent testament to the city's rich history and the confluence of cultures that have shaped its identity over the centuries. This grand palace, often referred to as the "Palace of the Normans," is a pinnacle of architectural magnificence, embodying the essence of Palermo's multicultural heritage.

Architectural Marvel and Cultural Crossroads

The Palazzo dei Normanni's story dates back to the 9th century, when the Arabs established the palace as their seat of power during their rule over Palermo. With the Norman conquest in the 11th century, the palace witnessed an era of transformation. The Normans, renowned for their affinity for adopting and adapting local traditions, embraced Palermo's diverse influences, fostering a unique blend of architectural styles that would come to define the palace's character.

Cappella Palatina: A Jewel Within the Palace

At the heart of the Palazzo dei Normanni lies the Cappella Palatina, a jewel of artistic achievement that encapsulates the multicultural spirit of Palermo. The chapel's walls and ceilings are adorned with a breathtaking mosaic cycle, reflecting Norman, Byzantine, and Arab influences. Scenes from the Bible come to life in a radiant symphony of colors and intricate details, creating an atmosphere that transcends time and place.

Architectural Fusion and Symbolism

The architecture of the Palazzo dei Normanni is a mosaic of history. Arab arches, Norman stone structures, and Byzantine craftsmanship harmonize in a symphony of artistic brilliance. The palace's design not only reflects the multicultural society of Palermo but also carries symbolic meaning, portraying an aspiration for harmony among diverse cultures and traditions.

Preservation and Accessibility

Through the ages, the Palazzo dei Normanni has been meticulously preserved, allowing visitors to step into a world where history and art converge. Guided tours offer insight into the palace's history, architecture, and cultural significance. The treasures within, from the Cappella Palatina's mosaics to the Royal Apartments, offer a glimpse into the lives of rulers and the cultural exchanges that defined Palermo.

Quattro Canti (Four Corners)

At the crossroads of Palermo's historical heart, the Quattro Canti, or Four Corners, emerges as a magnificent embodiment of the city's grandeur and artistic sophistication. This octagonal intersection, a jewel of Baroque urban design, stands as a resplendent testimony to the creative spirit and cultural heritage that define Palermo.

Architectural Marvel: An Intersection of Symmetry

The Quattro Canti is a symmetrical marvel where two main streets intersect at right angles. Each of the four facades represents a cardinal direction and celebrates a specific Spanish king, a season, and a patron saint. Elaborate statues, fountains, and decorative details adorn the facades, creating an immersive tableau of artistic opulence.

Baroque Extravagance: Theatrical Splendor

The Baroque style, characterized by its exuberance and theatricality, finds its zenith in the Quattro Canti. The facades are adorned with ornate stucco work, intricate sculptures, and exquisite reliefs that depict various allegorical figures and historical themes. The intersection is a living gallery, inviting contemplation and admiration.

Cultural Symbolism: Palermo's Identity in Stone

The Quattro Canti goes beyond architectural beauty; it embodies Palermo's identity. It speaks of the city's historical connections, artistic achievements, and cultural diversity. The statues symbolize virtues, arts, seasons, and even the winds that sweep across the Mediterranean, echoing the intertwining currents of Palermo's past and present.

The Passage of Time: A Witness to Palermo's History

As the city evolved, the Quattro Canti witnessed Palermo's changing landscape. It stood witness to political shifts, social changes, and the passage of time, offering a silent testament to the continuity of the city's identity despite the shifting currents of history.

Preserving Heritage: An Ongoing Legacy

The Quattro Canti has been meticulously preserved, allowing visitors to step into a Baroque masterpiece that captures Palermo's essence. It is a backdrop for strolling, reflecting, and engaging with the city's history through its intricate design and cultural symbolism.

Teatro Massimo

Dominating Palermo's skyline with its grandeur and artistic significance, the Teatro Massimo stands as a testament to the city's commitment to culture, creativity, and architectural innovation. This imposing opera house, renowned for its exceptional acoustics and exquisite design, embodies Palermo's vibrant cultural renaissance and enduring appreciation for the arts.

Architectural Splendor: A Monument to Opera

The Teatro Massimo's architectural magnificence is nothing short of awe-inspiring. Constructed in the late 19th century, it showcases a blend of architectural styles, including neoclassical and neobaroque elements. Its façade, adorned with sculptures and decorative details, reflects the city's aspiration to create a venue befitting its rich operatic tradition.

Acoustic Marvel: Resonance of Excellence

One of the Teatro Massimo's most renowned features is its exceptional acoustics. This hall has hosted countless opera performances, symphonies, and ballets, providing an intimate connection between artists and audiences. The auditorium's design ensures that every note resonates with precision and clarity, elevating the experience of live performances.

Cultural Renaissance: A Hub of Artistic Expression

The Teatro Massimo's inauguration marked Palermo's cultural revival, symbolizing the city's resurgence as a cultural hub. It became a platform for world-class performers, composers, and artists, attracting international attention and fostering a sense of pride among the Palermitani.

Guided Tours and Immersive Experiences

Visitors to the Teatro Massimo can embark on guided tours that take them through its opulent interiors, including the auditorium, royal box, and backstage areas. These tours provide insights into the theater's history, architecture, and the artists who have graced its stage.

Cultural Events and Modern Significance

Today, the Teatro Massimo continues to be a beacon of cultural significance. It hosts a diverse range of performances, from opera to concerts, offering both classical and contemporary experiences. It's also a venue for cultural festivals, workshops, and events that celebrate the arts and promote creative dialogue.

Norman Cathedral of Palermo

The Norman Cathedral of Palermo, an architectural masterpiece at the heart of the city, beckons travelers to immerse themselves in the layers of history, faith, and artistry that have shaped Palermo's identity. This cathedral, with its intricate blend of architectural styles, stands as a living testament to the city's rich past and its enduring cultural significance.

Architectural Tapestry: A Fusion of Styles

The Norman Cathedral is a living canvas that portrays Palermo's historical evolution. Its architecture reflects a synthesis of Norman, Arab, Byzantine, and Gothic styles, each contributing to the cathedral's unique character. The structure's harmonious diversity symbolizes Palermo's role as a cultural crossroads.

Palermo's Crown Jewel: Royal Tombs and Treasure

Within the cathedral lies a repository of history—Royal Tombs that house the remains of monarchs and figures integral to Sicilian history. Among these tombs, that of Roger II stands out—a testament to the Norman dynasty's impact on the region. The cathedral's treasury further showcases precious artifacts that underscore Palermo's connection to various civilizations.

The Norman Influence: Architecture and Ornamentation

The cathedral's Norman influence is evident in its exterior and interior, with elements such as the Norman-Byzantine façade and the triple-arched portico. The ornamental details, including decorative stonework and mosaics, provide insight into the artistic ingenuity of the era.

Gothic Additions: The Influence of Time

The Gothic additions, including the central nave and pointed arches, harmoniously coexist with the cathedral's earlier architectural elements. This evolution of styles echoes Palermo's capacity to embrace change while preserving its historical foundations.

Preserving the Past: A Reflection of Palermo's Values

The preservation of the Norman Cathedral reflects Palermo's commitment to safeguarding its heritage. The cathedral's role as a religious and cultural institution ensures that it remains a focal point for both locals and visitors to engage with the city's history.

Guided Exploration: Unveiling the Narrative

Guided tours of the cathedral offer a deeper understanding of its historical and artistic significance. Visitors can explore the cathedral's interiors, marvel at its mosaics, and appreciate the skill and craftsmanship that have gone into its creation and preservation.

Catacombe dei Cappuccini (Capuchin Catacombs)

Beneath the bustling streets of Palermo lies an extraordinary and solemn place—the Catacombe dei Cappuccini, or Capuchin Catacombs. This enigmatic site offers a distinctive perspective on the interplay between life, death, and artistic expression. It stands as a testament to Palermo's historical burial customs and its approach to commemorating the departed.

A Place of Reverence and Reflection

The Catacombe dei Cappuccini, established in the 16th century, was intended as a final resting place for the city's devout. Here, the bodies of the deceased were preserved through a meticulous process that involved mummification. The catacombs, originally intended for the Capuchin friars, eventually became a repository for the remains of the city's residents from various walks of life.

Mortuary Artistry: A Visual Journey through Time

Walking through the catacombs is like stepping into history. The mummified bodies, dressed in period attire, offer a silent testimony to the lives they once lived. Each preserved figure becomes a window into Palermo's past, providing insight into clothing, social status, and even causes of death.

Symbolism and Contemplation: A Unique Experience

The Capuchin Catacombs are not merely a display of preserved bodies; they are a meditation on the passage of time, the fragility of life, and the enduring human quest for remembrance. The juxtaposition of mortality and artistry creates an environment that prompts contemplation and reflection.

Cultural Curiosity: An Unconventional Perspective

While visiting the Catacombe dei Cappuccini may evoke a mix of emotions, it is an opportunity to engage with Palermo's historical practices and explore a facet of its past that is unique and thought-provoking. The catacombs offer an unconventional yet valuable insight into how different cultures have approached death and commemoration.

Preservation and Ethical Considerations

The preservation of the Catacombe dei Cappuccini raises ethical questions about the display of human remains. The site is an example of how different eras and societies have grappled with the preservation of memory and the human body. Guided tours help contextualize the site's historical and cultural significance.

Zisa Palace

The Zisa Palace, known as "Castello della Zisa" in Italian, is an intriguing historical site located in Palermo, Sicily, Italy. It is a remarkable architectural gem with a rich history. Here are some key details about the Zisa Palace:

Location:

The Zisa Palace is situated in the western part of Palermo, not far from the city center. It's part of the larger "Parco della Zisa" complex, which includes gardens and other historical buildings.

Architectural Style:

The Zisa Palace is a prime example of Islamic-influenced architecture. It showcases a fusion of European and Arab design elements, reflecting the Norman era when it was constructed.

Construction Date:

The palace was built in the 12th century during the reign of King William I of Sicily, also known as William the Bad. It served as a royal residence and a symbol of Norman power in Sicily.

Name Origin:

The name "Zisa" is believed to have Arabic origins, possibly derived from the Arabic word "aziz," meaning "splendid" or "noble." This name reflects the palace's elegance and grandeur.

Architecture and Design:

The Zisa Palace is characterized by its cubic shape, which is a common feature of Islamic architecture. It features ornate Arabic-style decorative elements, including intricate stucco work, geometric patterns, and decorative tiles.

Water Features:

The palace was designed with an ingenious hydraulic system that supplied water to its gardens and fountains. The use of water was not only functional but also added to the aesthetic beauty of the palace.

Purpose:

The Zisa Palace was used for various purposes over the centuries, including as a royal residence, a hunting lodge, and later as a military barracks. Today, it serves as a historical and cultural site.

Restoration:

Like many historical sites, the Zisa Palace has undergone restoration efforts to preserve its architectural features and historical significance.

Museum:

The palace now houses the Museo della Zisa, which features artifacts related to the history of Palermo and Sicily. Visitors can explore the museum's collections and learn more about the palace's history.

Surroundings:

The Zisa Palace is set within the Parco della Zisa, a green oasis in the city where visitors can enjoy gardens, sculptures, and other historical buildings, including the nearby Cuba Palace.

La Cuba

La Cuba is a historic palace located in Palermo, Sicily, Italy. It is known for its unique architectural style and historical significance. Here are some key details about La Cuba:

Location:

La Cuba is situated in the western part of Palermo, not far from the city center. It is located in the same vicinity as the Zisa Palace and the Parco della Zisa complex.

Construction Date:

La Cuba was built during the Norman period in the 12th century. It was commissioned by King William I of Sicily, also known as William the Bad. Like the nearby Zisa Palace, it served as a royal residence during this era.

Architectural Style:

The architectural style of La Cuba is characterized by its unique blend of Norman and Islamic influences. It features distinct Arabic-style decorative elements, including intricate stucco work, geometric patterns, and arches.

Design:

The palace is known for its cube-shaped design, which is reminiscent of Islamic architecture. The name "Cuba" is believed to be derived from the Arabic word "qubba," which means dome, possibly referring to a dome that was once part of the palace's design.

Use Over the Centuries:

Over the centuries, La Cuba has served various purposes, including as a royal residence, a hunting lodge, and a military barracks. Its rich history reflects the changing roles and influences in Sicilian history.

Restoration:

Like many historical sites, La Cuba has undergone restoration efforts to preserve its architectural features and historical significance. These efforts have helped maintain the palace's cultural and historical value.

Museum:

At certain points in its history, La Cuba has been used as a museum. However, its exact use may vary depending on the period and ongoing restoration efforts.

Surroundings:

La Cuba is located near the Zisa Palace and is part of the Parco della Zisa complex. The park and its surroundings offer a tranquil and historic atmosphere that contrasts with the bustling city.

Vucciria Market

The Vucciria Market, often referred to simply as "La Vucciria," is a historic and bustling street market located in the heart of Palermo, Sicily, Italy. Here are some key details about this vibrant market:

Location:

The Vucciria Market is situated in the historic center of Palermo, one of the city's oldest neighborhoods. It is easily accessible and is a central point for both locals and tourists.

History:

The market has a long history dating back centuries. Its name is believed to be derived from the Sicilian word "bucceria," which means confusion or chaos. The name reflects the lively and chaotic atmosphere that often characterizes street markets.

Market Days and Hours:

The Vucciria Market typically operates in the morning and early afternoon, with its busiest hours being around lunchtime. It is generally open from Monday to Saturday, although specific hours may vary.

Products:

The market offers a wide variety of products, including fresh produce, seafood, meats, cheeses, vegetables, fruits, spices, and Sicilian specialties. You can also find clothing, household goods, and traditional Sicilian street food.

Street Food:

Vucciria is renowned for its street food vendors, offering a range of Sicilian delights such as arancini (rice balls), panelle (chickpea fritters), sfincione (Sicilian pizza), and cannoli (sweet pastries filled with ricotta cheese).

Local Culture:

Visiting Vucciria provides an opportunity to immerse yourself in the local culture and experience the vibrant and authentic atmosphere of a traditional Sicilian market. The market is known for its lively and colorful ambiance.

Historical Landmarks:

The market is surrounded by historical landmarks and narrow alleyways, making it an excellent starting point for exploring the historic center of Palermo. Nearby attractions include churches, palaces, and squares.

Artistic Connections:

Vucciria has also been celebrated in literature and art. It was famously depicted by Italian painter Renato Guttuso in his painting "La Vucciria."

Changing Landscape:

While Vucciria remains a popular market, it has evolved over the years. It has faced challenges from modern supermarkets, but its enduring appeal lies in its authenticity and traditional offerings.

Fontana Pretoria (Pretoria Fountain)

The Fontana Pretoria, also known as the Pretoria Fountain, is one of Palermo's most famous and impressive landmarks. Here are some key details about this magnificent fountain:

Location:

The Fontana Pretoria is located in the heart of Palermo, specifically in the Piazza Pretoria, which is also known as the Piazza della Vergogna (Square of Shame). It's easily accessible and is a central point for exploring the city.

History:

The fountain was constructed in Florence, Italy, in the 16th century (between 1554 and 1555) by Francesco Camilliani. It was originally commissioned by the Spanish Viceroy of Sicily, Pedro Álvarez de Toledo, for a garden in Florence. However, it was later purchased by the city of Palermo and transported to Sicily.

Design:

The Fontana Pretoria is renowned for its elaborate and intricate design. It is a prime example of Renaissance art and features a circular basin surrounded by tiers of sculpted figures and ornate decorations. The fountain is often described as a "fountain of shame" due to the numerous nude statues adorning it.

Statues:

The fountain is adorned with numerous statues representing mythological figures, including nymphs, tritons, and gods. These statues are in various poses and depict scenes from Greek mythology. The statues are known for their detailed craftsmanship and artistic beauty.

Allegorical Themes:

In addition to the mythological figures, the Fontana Pretoria also features allegorical representations of the seasons, virtues, and vices. These statues and themes add depth and symbolism to the fountain's design.

Restorations:

Over the years, the Fontana Pretoria has undergone several restorations to preserve its beauty. It has faced weathering and pollution, but efforts have been made to maintain its original splendor.

Tourist Attraction:

Today, the Fontana Pretoria is a popular tourist attraction in Palermo. Visitors are often captivated by its grandeur and the skillful craftsmanship of the statues and decorations.

Surroundings:

The fountain is surrounded by historic buildings, including the Palermo City Hall (Palazzo delle Aquile), which adds to the charm of the square. The contrast between the ornate fountain and the austere architecture of the city hall creates a unique atmosphere.

Events and Gatherings:

The Piazza Pretoria often hosts cultural events and gatherings, making it a vibrant and lively spot in the city. It's a great place to relax, people-watch, and appreciate the beauty of the Fontana Pretoria.

Castello di Cefalà Diana

The Castello di Cefalà Diana, also known simply as Cefalà Diana Castle, is a historic fortress located in the town of Cefalà Diana, which is situated in the province of Palermo in Sicily, Italy. Here are some key details about this castle:

Location:

The Castello di Cefalà Diana is located in the town of Cefalà Diana, which is approximately 65 kilometers (about 40 miles) southeast of Palermo, the capital city of Sicily. The town is nestled in the Madonie Mountains, providing picturesque views of the surrounding countryside.

History:

The castle has a long and storied history, dating back to the medieval period. It was originally constructed during the Norman era, likely in the 12th century. Like many castles in Sicily, it has seen various rulers and modifications over the centuries.

Architecture:

The castle features typical Norman architectural elements, such as robust stone construction and defensive walls. It was strategically positioned to oversee and protect the surrounding area.

Ownership:

The castle has changed hands multiple times throughout history. It was originally built by the Normans but has been owned and occupied by various noble families, including the Ventimiglia and Valguarnera families.

Restoration:

In recent years, there have been efforts to restore and preserve the Castello di Cefalà Diana. Restoration work has focused on maintaining its historical and architectural significance.

Visiting:

The castle is open to visitors, and it offers a glimpse into the medieval history of Sicily. Exploring its ruins, courtyards, and towers provides a sense of the strategic importance of castles in the region's history.

Scenic Surroundings:

The castle is set amid the beautiful landscapes of the Madonie Mountains. Visitors can enjoy scenic views of the countryside and take in the tranquility of the area.

Hiking:

The Madonie Mountains offer excellent hiking opportunities, and some trails lead to or pass by the Castello di Cefalà Diana. Hiking enthusiasts can combine a visit to the castle with outdoor adventures in the surrounding natural area.

Villa palagonia

Villa Palagonia is a historic villa located in Bagheria, a town in the metropolitan city of Palermo in Sicily, Italy. This villa is renowned for its eccentric and unique architecture, featuring a multitude of grotesque sculptures and statues that adorn its façade and gardens. Here are some key details about Villa Palagonia:

Location:

Villa Palagonia is situated in the town of Bagheria, which is located along the northern coast of Sicily, approximately 15 kilometers (about 9 miles) east of Palermo, the capital city of Sicily.

History:

The villa was built during the 18th century for the eccentric Prince of Palagonia, Francesco Ferdinando II Gravina, who had a fascination with the bizarre and the grotesque. It was designed by the architect Tommaso Napoli.

Architectural Features:

Villa Palagonia is known for its unusual and whimsical architectural elements. The exterior of the villa is adorned with over 70 statues, many of which are grotesque and comical in nature. These sculptures depict a variety of characters and creatures, including mythical beings, animals, and distorted human figures.

Gardens:

The villa is surrounded by extensive gardens, which are also decorated with peculiar statues and sculptures. The gardens provide a serene and picturesque backdrop for visitors exploring the villa.

Eccentricity:

The villa's architecture reflects the Prince of Palagonia's eccentric tastes and sense of humor. It is said that he incorporated grotesque elements to challenge the norms of beauty and aesthetics.

Visiting:

Villa Palagonia is open to the public, and visitors can explore the villa's interior and gardens. It provides a unique and intriguing experience for those interested in art, history, and architectural eccentricity.

Cultural Events:

The villa occasionally hosts cultural events, exhibitions, and concerts, adding to its appeal as a cultural and historical attraction.

Film Location:

Villa Palagonia has been featured in various films and television productions due to its distinctive and captivating appearance.

Nearby Attractions:

Bagheria is known for its historical villas, and visitors to Villa Palagonia may also explore other nearby villas, such as Villa Cattolica and Villa Valguarnera.

MUSEUMS AND ART GALLERIES

Palermo's museums of history are more than mere repositories of artifacts; they are portals that transport you through time, allowing you to immerse yourself in the rich tapestry of the city's past and present. In 2023 and beyond, these museums beckon you to explore the stories, artifacts, and cultural heritage that have shaped Palermo's identity, inviting you on a journey of discovery and connection.

Palazzo dei Normanni Museum

Nestled within the walls of the illustrious Palazzo dei Normanni, the museum invites you on a captivating journey through Palermo's aristocratic past. In the year 2023 and beyond, as you step into the opulent halls of this historic palace, you're not just entering a museum—you're stepping into a realm of grandeur, power, and cultural significance that has shaped the identity of Palermo.

A Royal Residence Through Time

The Palazzo dei Normanni, also known as the Royal Palace, stands as a testament to the enduring influence of various civilizations on Palermo's architecture and history. From its origins as a fortress during the Arab rule to its transformation into a royal residence by the Normans, the palazzo carries the echoes of centuries of conquest and cultural fusion.

Cappella Palatina: A Jewel of Multicultural Artistry

At the heart of the Palazzo dei Normanni lies the Cappella Palatina, a true jewel of art and architecture. Stepping into this masterpiece is like entering a sanctuary where Norman, Byzantine, and Arab influences seamlessly intertwine. The intricate mosaics, intricate wooden decorations, and architectural details tell the story of Palermo's multicultural heritage, where diverse civilizations converged to create something breathtakingly beautiful.

A Glimpse into Aristocratic Life

The museum within the Palazzo dei Normanni allows you to delve into the world of Palermo's aristocracy. As you explore its chambers, adorned with frescoes, tapestries, and sumptuous décor, you'll gain insights into the lifestyles and aspirations of the city's nobility. The halls that once hosted royal courts and grand ceremonies come alive with the whispers of history.

The Evolution of Power

The museum doesn't just showcase opulence; it reflects the evolution of power dynamics that have shaped Palermo's history. From the days of Norman kings to subsequent rulers, the palazzo's history mirrors the political and cultural changes that have left an indelible mark on the city.

Cultural Significance and Identity

The Palazzo dei Normanni Museum isn't just a repository of artifacts; it's a reflection of Palermo's identity—a city that has embraced the influences of different civilizations while maintaining its unique character. The museum's exhibits, from ornate furnishings to historical documents, weave together the narrative of a city that has navigated the complexities of history with resilience and grace.

Museo Archeologico Regionale

Deep within the heart of Palermo lies the Museo Archeologico Regionale, a treasure trove that invites you to embark on a captivating journey through the ages. In the year 2023 and beyond, as you step into its hallowed halls, you're not just entering a museum; you're immersing yourself in the intricate tapestry of Sicily's past—a narrative woven by ancient civilizations and vibrant cultures.

A Mosaic of Civilizations

The Museo Archeologico Regionale is a living testament to Sicily's role as a crossroads of civilizations. With artifacts spanning from prehistoric times to the Middle Ages, the museum offers a comprehensive insight into the island's diverse and complex history. Each exhibit tells a story, revealing the unique contributions of Phoenicians, Greeks, Romans, and others who have left their mark on the island's cultural landscape.

Phoenician and Punic Legacy

The museum's collection includes rare and fascinating artifacts from Phoenician and Punic settlements that once thrived along the coast. These artifacts provide insights into the maritime trade, craftsmanship, and religious practices of these ancient cultures. You'll find objects that span from intricate jewelry to elaborate funerary offerings—each a testament to the lives and aspirations of those who inhabited the region.

Greek and Roman Splendors

The influence of Greek and Roman civilizations is palpable within the museum's exhibits. From captivating sculptures and pottery to intricate mosaics, these artifacts showcase the artistic mastery and societal values of these influential cultures. The museum's halls transport you to a world where gods and heroes coexist with everyday life.

Indigenous Cultures and Local Heritage

The museum doesn't just celebrate foreign influences; it also pays homage to the island's indigenous cultures. Artifacts from ancient indigenous civilizations provide a glimpse into the daily lives, rituals, and beliefs of Sicily's earliest inhabitants, forging a connection with the island's roots that's both enlightening and humbling.

Narratives of Identity and Resilience

Through its exhibits, the Museo Archeologico Regionale weaves a narrative of Sicily's identity—a tapestry shaped by centuries of cultural exchange, conquests, and challenges. The museum's role isn't just to preserve artifacts; it's to preserve the memory of the island's resilience and ability to adapt and thrive in the face of change.

Museo Internazionale delle Marionette Antonio Pasqualino

In the heart of Palermo, a captivating realm of art and entertainment awaits you at the Museo Internazionale delle Marionette Antonio Pasqualino. Stepping into this museum in 2023 and beyond is like entering a magical world where puppets come to life, bridging the gap between cultures, storytelling, and artistic expression—a journey that transcends time and invites you to rediscover the wonder of puppetry.

Puppets as Cultural Ambassadors

The museum celebrates puppetry as more than just a form of entertainment—it's a cultural bridge that connects people across borders. As you explore its exhibitions, you'll encounter an array of puppets from different countries and traditions. From intricate marionettes to shadow puppets, each figure tells a unique story that reflects the heritage, folklore, and artistic traditions of its origin.

A Glimpse into History

Puppetry has deep historical roots that stretch back through centuries. The museum's exhibits showcase the evolution of puppetry, from its origins in ancient rituals to its role as a popular form of entertainment. As you trace the history of puppets, you'll uncover the threads that tie together different cultures and eras, offering insights into the human desire for storytelling and connection.

Cultural Preservation and Revival

The museum's dedication to preserving and reviving traditional puppetry is evident in its exhibits and performances. Through workshops, demonstrations, and educational programs, the museum ensures that puppetry remains a vibrant and living art form. Its commitment to cultural heritage serves as an inspiration for preserving the cultural legacies that define our identities.

Global Exchange and Artistic Expression

Puppetry transcends language barriers, allowing artists to convey emotions, narratives, and ideas through movement and gesture. The museum showcases the global exchange of artistic ideas and techniques, highlighting the influence of different cultures on puppet design, performance styles, and storytelling traditions.

Pasqualino's Legacy

The museum is named after Antonio Pasqualino, a visionary puppeteer who dedicated his life to the art of puppetry and its cultural significance. His passion and dedication have left an indelible mark on the museum, serving as an inspiration for future generations of puppeteers, artists, and cultural enthusiasts.

Museo delle Maioliche Stanze al Genio

Within the embrace of Palermo lies the Museo delle Maioliche Stanze al Genio, a hidden sanctuary that invites you to discover the intricate beauty of ceramic artistry. As you step into this museum in 2023 and beyond, you're entering a world where vibrant colors, intricate patterns, and exquisite craftsmanship come together to create a tapestry that reflects Palermo's artistic legacy.

A Treasure Trove of Ceramics

The museum's collection is a visual feast of maiolica ceramics—vessels that have adorned homes, palaces, and courtyards for centuries. Each piece is a canvas that showcases the creativity and artistic mastery of generations past. From intricate plates and bowls to decorative tiles and vases, the maiolica ceramics are a testament to the enduring allure of this artistic medium.

Palermo's Aesthetic Legacy

The museum's exhibits provide insights into Palermo's aesthetic heritage—a fusion of cultural influences that have shaped the city's artistic identity. The ceramics bear witness to the convergence of different civilizations, from Moorish and Islamic designs to European motifs, resulting in an eclectic blend that's uniquely Palermo.

The Magic of Maiolica

Maiolica ceramics are more than just objects; they are carriers of stories and emotions. As you admire the delicate brushstrokes and intricate patterns, you're connecting with the artists' visions and the cultural currents that inspired their work. The museum's collection captures the essence of Palermo's artistic soul—a soul that has thrived through creativity, innovation, and the desire to beautify the everyday.

Palace Turned Museum

The museum's setting within a historic residence adds to its enchantment. The Stanze al Genio was once a private palace, and its transformation into a museum has preserved its elegant atmosphere while opening its doors to those who seek artistic inspiration. The juxtaposition of historical architecture and vibrant ceramics creates an ambiance that's both charming and inviting.

Cultural Continuity and Heritage

The Museo delle Maioliche Stanze al Genio isn't just a collection of ceramics; it's a living testament to Palermo's commitment to preserving its artistic heritage. Through the centuries, these ceramics have adorned homes, witnessed events, and contributed to the aesthetic fabric of the city. The museum ensures that this heritage continues to shine brightly, inspiring present and future generations.

Cantieri Culturali alla Zisa

In the vibrant heart of Palermo, the Cantieri Culturali alla Zisa stands as a dynamic cultural hub—a place where creativity, innovation, and the preservation of traditions converge. As you step into this multifaceted complex in 2023 and beyond, you're entering a space that celebrates the interplay between history and modernity, offering a glimpse into Palermo's evolving cultural landscape.

A Fusion of the Past and Present

The Cantieri Culturali alla Zisa is a testament to Palermo's ability to repurpose historic spaces for contemporary use. The complex was once a former industrial site, and its transformation into a cultural center has breathed new life into its halls and courtyards. This juxtaposition of history and modernity reflects Palermo's capacity to adapt while honoring its heritage.

A Canvas for Artistic Expression

The complex houses a variety of cultural spaces, including galleries, studios, theaters, and exhibition areas. It serves as a canvas where artists, both local and international, can showcase their creative visions. Through contemporary art exhibitions, performances, and cultural events, the Cantieri Culturali alla Zisa fosters a dialogue between different artistic expressions and audiences.

Preserving Tradition through Innovation

While celebrating the new, the complex also pays homage to Palermo's traditional cultural forms. Folk music, dance, and craft traditions find a place within its walls, showcasing the resilience of cultural practices that have stood the test of time. The complex serves as a bridge, connecting heritage with innovation and creating a platform for the coexistence of old and new.

A Catalyst for Interaction

The Cantieri Culturali alla Zisa serves as a catalyst for interaction and engagement. Its diverse offerings attract a cross-section of visitors, from locals seeking cultural enrichment to tourists eager to explore Palermo's artistic scene. The complex's workshops, lectures, and events provide opportunities for cross-cultural dialogue and the exchange of ideas.

A Vibrant Expression of Identity

The complex isn't just a collection of spaces; it's a reflection of Palermo's identity—a city that values its history, embraces contemporary creativity, and fosters an atmosphere of inclusivity. The Cantieri Culturali alla Zisa embodies Palermo's spirit of resilience, adaptability, and its unwavering commitment to celebrating its cultural wealth.

Etnografico Siciliano Museum

Deep within the heart of Palermo, the Museo Etnografico Siciliano awaits—a sanctuary that invites you to explore the intricate layers of Sicilian culture. In the year 2023 and beyond, as you step into this museum, you're not just entering a space filled with artifacts; you're embarking on a journey that delves into the traditions, stories, and way of life that define the essence of Sicily.

Cultural Portraits of Sicily

The Museo Etnografico Siciliano is a collection of cultural portraits that capture the diversity and complexity of the island's identity. Through its exhibits, you'll encounter artifacts that reflect the rhythms of rural life, the vitality of urban centers, and the resilience of communities that have thrived in the face of change.

Exploring Everyday Life

The museum offers a glimpse into the everyday lives of Sicilians throughout history. From traditional clothing and crafts to agricultural tools and domestic implements, the artifacts tell stories of work, family, and community—providing insights into the values and practices that have shaped Sicilian society.

Celebrating Festivals and Traditions

Sicily's festivals and traditions are deeply woven into its cultural fabric. The museum's exhibits highlight the vibrant celebrations, religious processions, and rituals that mark the passage of time. Through masks, costumes, and ceremonial objects, you'll gain a deeper understanding of the role these events play in preserving identity and fostering community bonds.

Harmony of Multicultural Influences

Sicily's history as a cultural crossroads is reflected in the museum's exhibits. Arab, Norman, Spanish, and other influences have left an indelible mark on the island's traditions and way of life. The artifacts showcase the harmonious blend of cultures that have shaped Sicily's artistic expressions, culinary traditions, and daily practices.

Palazzo Abatellis

In the heart of Palermo stands the resplendent Palazzo Abatellis, a testament to the city's rich artistic heritage and cultural legacy. In the year 2023 and beyond, as you enter this magnificent palace, you're not just stepping into a museum;

you're embarking on a captivating journey through time, where art becomes a window into the soul of Palermo.

A Palatial Canvas

Palazzo Abatellis is a masterpiece in itself—a palatial canvas that encapsulates the evolution of architectural styles from the Gothic to the Renaissance. Its grandeur sets the stage for an encounter with artistic treasures that have been meticulously preserved and curated within its walls.

The Galleria Regionale della Sicilia

The heart of Palazzo Abatellis is the Galleria Regionale della Sicilia, a treasure trove of artworks that celebrate Sicilian artistic achievements from the Middle Ages to the Baroque period. The gallery showcases an array of paintings, sculptures, and decorative arts that offer a glimpse into the artistic evolution of Palermo and the island as a whole.

Masterpieces and Innovations

Among the remarkable artworks, you'll encounter masterpieces that capture the essence of their time. From Antonello da Messina's celebrated "Annunciation" to Renaissance and Baroque sculptures and paintings, the collection mirrors the city's ability to embrace artistic innovations while preserving its cultural roots.

Echoes of Sicilian Identity

The artworks within Palazzo Abatellis resonate with the echoes of Sicilian identity. Scenes of everyday life, religious devotion, and historical events reveal the narratives that have shaped the island's character. The art becomes a mirror reflecting the interplay of cultures, faiths, and traditions that define Palermo.

A Feast for the Senses

Beyond the visual splendors, Palazzo Abatellis engages the senses in its architectural details and atmospheric courtyards. The interplay of light and shadow, the sound of footsteps on ancient stone floors, and the fragrant breezes that waft through its open spaces create an immersive experience that enriches your connection to the artworks.

A Cultural Sanctuary

Palazzo Abatellis isn't merely a museum; it's a sanctuary where art and history intersect. The palace's role goes beyond preservation—it's a vessel that transports you through centuries of creativity, aspiration, and cultural exchange.

Modern Art at GAM Palermo

In the heart of Palermo, the GAM Palermo stands as a beacon of modern artistic expression—a dynamic space that invites you to explore the ever-evolving landscape of contemporary creativity. In the year 2023 and beyond, as you step into this museum, you're not just entering a gallery; you're immersing yourself in a world where innovation, diversity, and thought-provoking concepts intertwine to shape Palermo's modern artistic identity.

A Haven for Contemporary Art

GAM Palermo serves as a haven for contemporary artists and their visions. Its galleries showcase a diverse range of artworks, from paintings and sculptures to multimedia installations and performance art. This space is a canvas where artists challenge conventions, experiment with materials, and engage with society's pressing issues.

A Dialogue with the Present

The museum's collection reflects the pulse of our times. Artworks presented within its walls offer a dialogue with contemporary issues, social narratives, and cultural shifts. As you engage with these pieces, you're participating in a conversation that spans across borders, generations, and perspectives—a conversation that resonates with the complexities of modern life.

Championing Innovation and Experimentation

GAM Palermo is a testament to the power of artistic innovation. The museum nurtures the avant-garde, providing a platform for emerging talents to push boundaries and experiment with new forms of expression. Through ever-evolving exhibitions and projects, the museum keeps its finger on the pulse of contemporary creativity.

Cultural Diversity and Pluralism

The museum's commitment to cultural diversity is palpable in its programming. International artists find their place alongside local creators, creating a rich tapestry of ideas and influences. This diversity mirrors Palermo's character as a city that embraces multiculturalism and celebrates the exchange of artistic perspectives.

Engaging Audiences and Provoking Thought

GAM Palermo goes beyond being a static display—it's an interactive space that engages audiences in thought-provoking ways. Interactive installations, performances, and workshops invite visitors to question, reflect, and participate in the creative process, fostering a deeper connection to the art and its significance.

CATHEDRALS AND RELIGIOUS SITES

Palermo, a city steeped in history and spirituality, is adorned with cathedrals and religious sites that stand as testament to its cultural richness and devotion. In 2023 and beyond, as you explore these hallowed grounds, you'll be transported through time, tracing the footsteps of pilgrims, artisans, and believers who have left their mark on Palermo's religious heritage. Join us on a journey through sacred splendor, where architecture, artistry, and faith intertwine.

Cattedrale di Palermo

At the heart of Palermo's intricate tapestry lies the magnificent Cattedrale di Palermo, a grandeur emblem of the city's historical and cultural fusion. This awe-inspiring cathedral stands not only as a testament to faith but as a living monument that narrates the stories of Normans, Arabs, and generations of Palermitans who have contributed to its resplendent legacy. As you step into its hallowed halls in 2023 and beyond, you'll be transported through time, where the echoes of history resonate in every stone and arch.

A Marvel of Multicultural Synthesis

The Cattedrale di Palermo is a harmonious marriage of architectural styles, each layer bearing the mark of different civilizations. Its imposing exterior, characterized by Norman towers and Gothic spires, mirrors the city's dynamic history, where diverse cultures converged to create an architectural masterpiece that defies singular classification.

Gleaming Mosaics and Arab Influence

Upon entering the cathedral, your gaze is drawn to the breathtaking mosaics that adorn the apse. These intricate designs, rich with gold and vibrant colors, bear the unmistakable imprint of Arab craftsmanship. As you marvel at the beauty of these mosaics, you're reminded of Palermo's role as a crossroads where cultures intermingled to create something truly unique.

Royal Tombs and Testament to Nobility

Venture deeper into the cathedral and you'll encounter the royal tombs—a somber reminder of the noble dynasties that shaped Sicilian history. The tombs of Norman kings and other monarchs offer insight into their reigns, while the juxtaposition of different funerary styles reflects the cathedral's centuries-long evolution.

Chapels of Art and Devotion

The Cattedrale di Palermo also houses chapels that pay tribute to saints and religious devotion. The Chapel of Santa Rosalia, the city's patron saint, is a testament to Palermo's enduring faith, while the Chapel of the Crucifix houses the miraculous crucifix that is central to the city's religious celebrations.

A Living Legacy

Beyond its architectural grandeur, the Cattedrale di Palermo is a living testament to Palermo's resilience and adaptability. It's a symbol of a city that embraced diversity, a city that continues to evolve while preserving its rich heritage.

Cappella Palatina

Tucked within the historic confines of the Norman Palace, the Cappella Palatina stands as an exquisite testament to Palermo's multicultural heritage and artistic brilliance. As you step into this sacred space in 2023 and beyond, you'll be transported to a world where Byzantine mosaics, Arab motifs, and Norman architecture converge in a harmonious symphony of beauty and spirituality.

Byzantine Opulence and Arab Influence

The Cappella Palatina's interior is a living canvas adorned with captivating Byzantine mosaics that evoke a sense of divine splendor. These meticulously crafted works of art depict biblical scenes, adorned with intricate gold leaf and vivid colors, casting an ethereal glow that transports visitors to another realm. The Arab influence is evident in the horseshoe arches, geometric designs, and stucco decorations that adorn the walls and ceilings, creating a mesmerizing fusion of cultures.

Norman Grandeur and Spiritual Sanctuary

As your gaze ascends to the ornate wooden ceiling, you'll be struck by the Norman craftsmanship that completes this architectural marvel. The solid wooden beams are a stark yet harmonious contrast to the opulent mosaics, illustrating the convergence of strength and beauty that defines Palermo's history.

Religious Narratives and Harmony

The mosaics of the Cappella Palatina serve as visual narratives, capturing moments from biblical stories in intricate detail. The scenes, which include depictions of Christ's life and the apostles, transcend linguistic and cultural boundaries, serving as a universal expression of faith and spirituality.

A Treasure Trove of Timelessness

Every inch of the Cappella Palatina resonates with the echoes of history, where kings and emperors once prayed, and artists labored to create a space that transcends time. The intricacy of the artwork and the thoughtfulness of the design reflect the devotion and reverence that have marked this chapel as a beacon of Palermo's spiritual identity.

Inspirational Contemplation

The Cappella Palatina is more than a place of worship; it's a place of contemplation and inspiration. As you immerse yourself in its beauty, take a moment to reflect on the generations that have passed through its doors and the artistry that has transformed it into a sanctuary of human expression and divine connection.

San Giovanni degli Eremiti

Nestled within the heart of Palermo, the San Giovanni degli Eremiti is a place where time seems to stand still, offering a peaceful sanctuary amidst the bustling city. As you step into this historical gem in 2023 and beyond, you'll find yourself transported to an oasis of tranquility, where Norman architecture and Moorish influences meld to create a space of profound beauty and serenity.

A Tranquil Oasis

San Giovanni degli Eremiti is a testament to the timeless allure of simplicity. The gentle rustling of palm trees, the soothing trickling of fountains, and the scent of blooming flowers create an ambiance that's both serene and inviting. This hidden gem allows you to escape the demands of modern life and immerse yourself in a world of stillness and contemplation.

Moorish and Norman Fusion

The architectural design of San Giovanni degli Eremiti is a harmonious synthesis of Norman and Moorish styles. The red domes that crown the church are reminiscent of Arab architecture, creating a captivating contrast against the blue Sicilian sky. The simplicity of the church's facade belies the rich history and cultural interplay that have shaped it.

Whispers of History

As you explore the church's interior, you'll find that it's more than just a place of worship—it's a repository of history. The cloister, with its graceful arches and quiet courtyards, tells the story of the monks who once sought solace and inspiration within these walls. The Arabic inscriptions and geometric patterns that adorn the church's interiors are reminders of Palermo's historical connections with the Arab world.

An Invitation to Contemplate

San Giovanni degli Eremiti isn't merely a structure; it's an invitation to pause, reflect, and connect with the essence of the past. Whether you're exploring the cloisters, admiring the architecture, or simply sitting in quiet contemplation, you're enveloped in an atmosphere that encourages introspection and appreciation for the beauty of simplicity.

A Retreat for the Soul

In a world often characterized by noise and busyness, San Giovanni degli Eremiti stands as a refuge for the soul. It's a place where the whispers of history and the tranquility of nature combine to offer a respite from the outside world—a space to recharge, meditate, and find solace.

Oratorio di San Lorenzo

Amidst the vibrant streets of Palermo, the Oratorio di San Lorenzo stands as a hidden jewel that beckons travelers and locals alike to uncover its artistic treasures. In 2023 and beyond, as you step into this unassuming yet profoundly captivating space, you'll find yourself immersed in a world of intricate frescoes, delicate stucco work, and a profound sense of devotion that transcends time.

A Feast of Frescoes

The Oratorio di San Lorenzo is a testament to the power of art to communicate spirituality. Its walls are adorned with frescoes that vividly depict scenes from the Bible, each stroke of paint telling a story that resonates through the ages. The artwork is not just an aesthetic marvel; it's a gateway to understanding the faith and values that have shaped Palermo's history.

Meticulous Stucco Work

The stucco work that adorns the Oratorio di San Lorenzo is a testament to the craftsmanship of the artisans who dedicated their skills to this sacred space. Delicate floral patterns, intricate geometric designs, and elaborate frames create an atmosphere of beauty and reverence, enveloping visitors in an environment that's both exquisite and contemplative.

A Spiritual Journey

As you walk through the oratory, you'll find yourself on a spiritual journey guided by the artwork that lines the walls. Scenes from the lives of saints, the crucifixion of Christ, and other biblical narratives serve as points of reflection, inviting you to connect with the faith and devotion that have animated generations of believers.

A Hidden Gem with a Story

The unassuming exterior of the Oratorio di San Lorenzo belies the rich tapestry of history that resides within. This oratory, which once belonged to a lay brotherhood, encapsulates the essence of a community united by their faith. The very act of stepping into this space connects you with the stories of those who have sought solace and meaning within its walls.

A Sanctuary of Silence

In the midst of Palermo's bustling streets, the Oratorio di San Lorenzo offers a sanctuary of silence—a place to step away from the noise of everyday life and engage with the profound themes of existence, faith, and human connection. It's a reminder that even in the midst of a bustling city, there are pockets of stillness where the soul can find solace.

Santuario Santa Rosalia

High atop Monte Pellegrino, overlooking the city of Palermo, the Santuario Santa Rosalia stands as a beacon of faith, offering both pilgrims and visitors a place of solace, reflection, and breathtaking panoramic views. In the year 2023 and beyond, as you ascend to this sacred sanctuary, you'll embark on a spiritual journey that honors the patron saint of Palermo while immersing yourself in the natural beauty that surrounds it.

A Spiritual Pilgrimage

The journey to the Santuario Santa Rosalia is more than a physical ascent—it's a spiritual pilgrimage. As you make your way up the winding path, you'll be surrounded by the scent of Mediterranean flora, the song of birds, and the sense of anticipation that accompanies a meaningful journey. The trek is a symbolic reflection of the devotion that believers have shown for centuries.

A Tranquil Haven

Arriving at the sanctuary, you'll discover a haven of tranquility—a place where the world's demands seem to fade away. The serene atmosphere, coupled with the spectacular views of the city and sea, creates an environment that's conducive to introspection, prayer, and connecting with the divine.

The Story of Santa Rosalia

Inside the sanctuary, you'll encounter the story of Santa Rosalia, a hermit who lived in solitude and devoted her life to prayer and reflection. The cave where she found refuge is a testament to her commitment to spirituality. As you explore the sanctuary, you'll find chapels, altars, and artworks that pay homage to her life and the miraculous events associated with her devotion.

Panoramic Vistas and Contemplation

The panoramic views from the Santuario Santa Rosalia offer a unique perspective of Palermo and its surroundings. The city's rooftops, the glistening sea, and the expansive horizon serve as a backdrop for moments of deep contemplation. Whether you're gazing out toward the sea or meditating within the sanctuary, the connection between nature, spirituality, and the human soul becomes palpable.

A Symbol of Unity and Faith

Santuario Santa Rosalia is more than just a religious site; it's a symbol of Palermo's unity and faith. As you stand on this mountaintop, you're joining a legacy of believers who have sought inspiration, solace, and a sense of purpose in this sacred space.

La Martorana

Nestled within the vibrant streets of Palermo, the Church of Santa Maria dell'Ammiraglio, commonly known as La Martorana, emerges as a living testament to the city's rich history and the interplay of diverse cultures. This Byzantine-influenced gem stands as a beacon of Palermo's artistic heritage and reflects the harmonious fusion of architectural styles that define the city's identity.

Architectural Brilliance: Byzantine Aesthetics in Palermo

La Martorana's architectural design pays homage to the Byzantine traditions that shaped its construction. The church's stunning mosaics, intricate patterns, and ornate details capture the essence of Byzantine aesthetics, creating an ambiance of reverence and beauty that transcends time.

Mosaics That Tell Stories: A Glimpse into the Past

As you step into La Martorana, your gaze is immediately drawn to the resplendent mosaics that adorn its walls and dome. These mosaics depict scenes from the life of Christ, the Virgin Mary, and various saints, capturing the narrative of Christianity with an artistic eloquence that invites contemplation and admiration.

Arab-Byzantine Synthesis: Cultural Convergence in Stone

La Martorana's architectural features bear witness to Palermo's multicultural heritage. Its Arab-influenced arches, Norman-style capitals, and Byzantine-inspired domes create a harmonious synthesis that reflects the city's history of diverse cultural influences.

Historical Significance and Resilience

La Martorana has withstood the test of time, surviving historical shifts and cultural changes. Its journey through centuries serves as a poignant reminder of Palermo's ability to embrace its past while evolving with the present.

The Palatine Chapel

Nestled within the heart of the Palazzo dei Normanni, the Palatine Chapel stands as an exquisite jewel that encapsulates the cultural fusion and artistic brilliance of Palermo's history. This chapel, also known as Cappella Palatina, is a testament to the city's rich heritage, where Norman, Byzantine, and Arab influences harmoniously intertwine.

Architectural Marvel: Norman-Arab-Byzantine Synthesis

The Palatine Chapel is a masterpiece of architectural fusion. Its design incorporates the symmetrical layout of Norman architecture, the intricate mosaics of Byzantine tradition, and the geometric patterns and arches inspired by Arab aesthetics. This synthesis creates an environment of spiritual grandeur and artistic excellence.

Radiant Mosaics: Art in Every Detail

As you enter the Palatine Chapel, your eyes are immediately drawn to the walls and ceilings adorned with shimmering mosaics. These intricate artworks narrate scenes from the Bible, depicting the life of Christ, the Virgin Mary, and other biblical figures. The mosaics are a symphony of color and detail, offering a visual feast that engages the senses.

Cultural Crossroads: Echoes of History

The Palatine Chapel's mosaics are more than mere artworks; they are a reflection of Palermo's multicultural history. They reveal the city's role as a crossroads of civilizations, where artistic and spiritual traditions converged, resulting in a harmonious expression of faith and creativity.

Royal Connections: The Influence of Rulers

The chapel's creation was overseen by Roger II, a Norman ruler known for his appreciation of diverse cultures. The mosaics reflect his desire to assert his authority while embracing the cultural diversity of his kingdom, epitomizing the spirit of Palermo's historical rulers.

Preserving Beauty: A Glimpse into History

The meticulous preservation of the Palatine Chapel allows visitors to step back in time and experience the ambiance of a bygone era. Guided tours offer insights into the chapel's history, the stories depicted in its mosaics, and the artistic techniques that brought its beauty to life.

Spiritual Resonance: The Essence of Palermo

The Palatine Chapel is more than a place of worship; it's a living embodiment of Palermo's identity. It reflects the city's enduring commitment to embracing cultural diversity, fostering artistic excellence, and creating spaces that inspire both reverence and wonder.

Church of Saint John of the Hermits

The Church of Saint John of the Hermits, known as "Chiesa di San Giovanni degli Eremiti" in Italian, is a unique and historically significant church located in Palermo, Sicily, Italy. Here are some key details about this remarkable church:

Location:

The Church of Saint John of the Hermits is situated in the heart of Palermo, the capital city of Sicily. It is conveniently located and easily accessible to visitors exploring the city.

Architecture:

The church is celebrated for its distinctive architecture, which combines several different styles. It features a Norman-Arab design, characterized by its red-domed cupolas, cubic forms, and Islamic-inspired arches. This architectural fusion is a testament to the multicultural history of Sicily.

History:

The church's origins date back to the 6th century when it was founded by Byzantine monks. It underwent various renovations and additions over the centuries, with Norman influences introduced during the 12th century.

Cubic Design:

One of the most striking features of the Church of Saint John of the Hermits is its cube-like shape. This design, reminiscent of Islamic architecture, sets it apart from many other churches in Europe.

Courtyard:

The church is surrounded by a beautiful courtyard with lush greenery and palm trees. The courtyard provides a peaceful and scenic setting for visitors.

Interior:

Inside the church, visitors can admire the Norman-Arab architectural elements, including the pointed arches and dome. The interior is relatively simple compared to the exterior but retains its historical charm.

Historical Significance:

The Church of Saint John of the Hermits is not only architecturally significant but also historically important. It has witnessed centuries of Sicilian history and reflects the cultural exchanges and influences that have shaped the island.

Visiting:

The church is open to visitors, and it offers a glimpse into the unique architectural and historical heritage of Sicily. It is often included as a stop on tours of Palermo's historical and cultural sites.

Surroundings:

The church is located in a charming part of Palermo, near other historical landmarks and attractions, such as the Palazzo dei Normanni (Norman Palace) and the Palermo Botanical Garden.

STATUES AND MONUMENTS

Palermo, the capital city of Sicily, Italy, is rich in history and culture, and it boasts numerous statues and monuments that reflect its diverse heritage. Here is a guide to some of the most notable statues and monuments you can explore while visiting Palermo:

Statue of Carlo V

The Statue of Carlo V in Palermo, Italy, is an equestrian statue dedicated to the Holy Roman Emperor Charles V. Here are some key details about this statue:

Location:

The statue is located in Palermo, the capital city of Sicily, in Piazza Bologni, which is near the Palermo Cathedral (Cattedrale di Palermo).

Emperor Charles V:

Charles V, also known as Charles I of Spain, was a powerful monarch who ruled a vast empire in the 16th century, including Spain, parts of Italy, the Holy Roman Empire, and the Americas. He played a significant role in European politics during his reign.

History:

The statue of Carlo V was erected in 1631, long after Charles V's time. It was commissioned by the Viceroy of Sicily, Juan de la Cerda, to commemorate the emperor's visit to Palermo in 1535. The statue was created by the Flemish sculptor Giovanni van den Hoecke.

Equestrian Statue:

The statue features Charles V on horseback, a common motif for statues of monarchs and rulers. Charles is depicted in a regal pose, wearing armor and a crown, symbolizing his authority and power.

Symbolism:

The statue of Carlo V is a symbol of the historical ties between Sicily and the Spanish Habsburg dynasty, which ruled over Sicily during the 16th century.

Surroundings:

The statue stands in a square near the Palermo Cathedral, which is one of the city's most important religious landmarks.

The presence of the statue adds historical and cultural significance to this part of Palermo.

Restoration:

Like many historical monuments, the Statue of Carlo V has undergone restoration efforts over the years to preserve its historical and artistic value.

Tourism:

The statue is a notable attraction for visitors exploring the historic center of Palermo. It's a part of the city's rich tapestry of historical and artistic landmarks.

Statue of Ruggero Settimo

The Statue of Ruggero Settimo is a prominent monument located in Palermo, Italy, dedicated to Ruggero Settimo, a significant historical figure in Sicilian and Italian history. Here are some key details about this statue:

Location:

The Statue of Ruggero Settimo is situated in Piazza Ruggero Settimo, also known as Piazza Politeama. This central square is a hub of cultural and commercial activity in Palermo.

Ruggero Settimo:

Ruggero Settimo (1776–1863) was a Sicilian statesman and patriot who played a crucial role in the movement for Sicilian independence and Italian unification during the 19th century. He served as the President of the Kingdom of Sicily from 1830 to 1848.

Monument Design:

The statue is an imposing equestrian monument, depicting Ruggero Settimo on horseback. It is a classic representation of a leader in a noble and commanding pose.

Inscription:

The base of the statue typically includes an inscription commemorating Ruggero Settimo's contributions to Sicily and Italy's quest for unification.

Historical Significance:

Ruggero Settimo is celebrated for his efforts to modernize and reform Sicily during his presidency, as well as his support for Italian unification under the leadership of figures like Giuseppe Garibaldi.

Piazza Politeama:

The statue is a focal point in Piazza Politeama, a vibrant and lively square known for its theaters, shopping, and cultural events. It's a popular gathering place for both locals and tourists.

Cultural Events:

Piazza Politeama often hosts various cultural events, concerts, and festivals, making it an active and dynamic part of Palermo's social scene.

Restorations:

Like many historic monuments, the Statue of Ruggero Settimo has undergone restoration work over the years to preserve its appearance and historical significance.

Statue of Giuseppe Garibaldi

The Statue of Giuseppe Garibaldi is a notable monument in Palermo, Italy, dedicated to one of the key figures in the Italian unification (Risorgimento) movement. Here are some key details about this statue:

Location:

The statue of Giuseppe Garibaldi is located in Piazza Marina, a picturesque square in the heart of Palermo. This square is known for its historical significance and scenic beauty.

Giuseppe Garibaldi:

Giuseppe Garibaldi (1807–1882) was an Italian general and patriot who played a crucial role in the unification of Italy in the 19th century. He is revered for his military leadership and commitment to Italian unity.

Monument Design:

The statue is an equestrian monument, featuring Giuseppe Garibaldi mounted on a horse. He is depicted in a heroic and determined posture, reflecting his leadership in the struggle for Italian unification.

Inscription:

The base of the statue often includes an inscription or plaque commemorating Giuseppe Garibaldi's contributions to the unification of Italy.

Historical Significance:

Giuseppe Garibaldi is known for leading the famous "Expedition of the Thousand" (Spedizione dei Mille) in 1860, which aimed to liberate Sicily and southern Italy from Bourbon rule. His successful campaign contributed significantly to the unification of Italy.

Piazza Marina:

The statue is a central feature of Piazza Marina, a square surrounded by historic buildings, including the Palazzo Chiaramonte and the Church of Santa Maria della Catena. The square's tranquil atmosphere and beautiful greenery make it a delightful place for a leisurely stroll.

Cultural Events:

Piazza Marina occasionally hosts cultural events, art exhibitions, and festivals, making it a vibrant and dynamic space in Palermo.

Restorations:

Like many historic monuments, the Statue of Giuseppe Garibaldi has undergone restoration work to ensure its preservation and maintain its historical and artistic significance.

Statue of the Genius of Palermo (Il Genio di Palermo)

The Statue of the Genius of Palermo, known as "Il Genio di Palermo" in Italian, is a significant symbol of the city. Here are some key details about this statue:

Location:

The Statue of the Genius of Palermo is situated in Piazza Giulio Cesare, a square in the heart of Palermo, Italy. This square is commonly referred to as "Piazza Genio."

Symbolism:

The statue represents the mythical protector and guardian spirit of Palermo, often referred to as the "Genius of Palermo" or "Genius loci" (spirit of the place). It is a personification of the city's identity and cultural heritage.

Artistic Representation:

The statue typically depicts a young man holding a serpent, which is a prominent symbol associated with the Genius of Palermo. The serpent is often interpreted as a representation of the ancient myths and legends of Palermo.

Historical Significance:

The Genius of Palermo has deep historical and cultural roots in the city's heritage. It is a symbol of the city's unique character and the blend of various cultures that have influenced Palermo throughout its history, including Phoenician, Roman, Arab, Norman, and Spanish influences.

Surroundings:

Piazza Giulio Cesare and its surroundings are worth exploring. Nearby attractions include historic buildings, such as the Palazzo dei Normanni (Norman Palace), which houses the famous Palatine Chapel with its intricate mosaics.

Local Lore:

Local legends and folklore often revolve around the Genius of Palermo, emphasizing its protective role and connection to the city's history.

Cultural Significance:

The statue serves as a symbol of pride for the people of Palermo and is an integral part of the city's cultural identity.

Restorations:

Over the years, the Statue of the Genius of Palermo has undergone restoration work to preserve its artistic and historical value.

Statue of Santa Rosalia

The Statue of Santa Rosalia is a significant religious monument in Palermo, Italy, dedicated to the city's patron saint, Santa Rosalia. Here are some key details about this statue:

Location:

The Statue of Santa Rosalia is typically located in the Palermo Cathedral (Cattedrale di Palermo) or in the Cathedral Square (Piazza della Cattedrale), which is in the heart of Palermo.

Santa Rosalia:

Santa Rosalia is the patron saint of Palermo and is revered for her role in protecting the city. She is known for her religious devotion and her reputed intervention during a plague outbreak in the city in the 17th century.

Monument Design:

The statue of Santa Rosalia often depicts her in the attire of a nun or a religious figure, holding a cross, a skull, and sometimes a bouquet of flowers. These elements are symbolic of her life of piety and her connection to the city's history.

Historical Significance:

The cult of Santa Rosalia is deeply rooted in Palermo's history. Her image and story are associated with the city's religious and cultural identity.

Festival:

The Feast of Santa Rosalia, known as "Festa di Santa Rosalia" or "U Fistinu" in Sicilian dialect, is a major religious celebration in Palermo, typically held from July 10th to 15th each year. During this festival, the statue of Santa Rosalia is paraded through the streets of Palermo, and various religious and cultural events take place.

Religious Devotion:

The statue and the cult of Santa Rosalia continue to be an important focus of religious devotion for the people of

Palermo, who seek her intercession for various blessings and protection.

Palermo Cathedral:

If you visit the Palermo Cathedral, you can often find the statue of Santa Rosalia prominently displayed within the cathedral. The cathedral itself is a stunning architectural masterpiece and an important religious site in the city.

Devotional Art:

The statue is a representation of the rich tradition of devotional art in Palermo and serves as a reminder of the city's strong connection to its religious heritage.

Statue of Vincenzo Florio

The Statue of Vincenzo Florio is a significant monument in Palermo, Italy, dedicated to Vincenzo Florio, a prominent industrialist and entrepreneur who made significant contributions to the economic development of Sicily. Here are some key details about this statue:

Location:

The Statue of Vincenzo Florio is usually located in Villa Trabia, a park in Palermo. Villa Trabia is a historical park and garden that is often used for cultural events and public gatherings.

Vincenzo Florio:

Vincenzo Florio (1833–1899) was a Sicilian entrepreneur, industrialist, and philanthropist. He was a key figure in the economic and industrial development of Sicily during the late 19th century. He is particularly well-known for his contributions to the wine and tuna fishing industries in the region.

Monument Design:

The statue typically portrays Vincenzo Florio in a dignified and possibly period-appropriate attire. It may include inscriptions or plaques detailing his contributions and achievements.

Historical Significance:

Vincenzo Florio's entrepreneurial spirit and investments played a significant role in the development of Sicilian industries, particularly in the Marsala wine and tuna canning sectors. His business ventures had a positive impact on the region's economy and employment opportunities.

Philanthropy:

In addition to his business endeavors, Vincenzo Florio was known for his philanthropic activities, contributing to the well-being of the local community and supporting cultural and educational initiatives.

Cultural Events:

Villa Trabia, where the statue is located, often serves as a venue for cultural events, art exhibitions, and public gatherings. It is a serene and beautiful place within the city.

Restorations:

Like many historical monuments, the Statue of Vincenzo Florio may have undergone restoration work over the years to preserve its historical and artistic value.

Giuseppe verdi statue

Giuseppe Verdi (1813-1901) was one of the most influential and celebrated composers of Italian opera in the 19th century. He is known for his masterful compositions and contributions to the world of opera. Here are some key details about Giuseppe Verdi:

Early Life:

Verdi was born on October 9, 1813, in Le Roncole, a village in the Duchy of Parma, which is now part of Italy. He came from humble beginnings and showed an early aptitude for music.

Operatic Career:

Verdi composed numerous operas that became staples of the operatic repertoire. Some of his most famous works include "La Traviata," "Rigoletto," "Aida," "Nabucco," "Don Carlos," and "Otello," among others. His operas are known for their melodic richness, emotional depth, and dramatic storytelling.

Italian Nationalism:

Verdi lived during a period of Italian nationalism and political upheaval. His operas often contained themes of patriotism and resistance to foreign rule, making him a symbol of the Italian unification movement known as the Risorgimento.

Personal Tragedies:

Verdi experienced personal tragedies, including the deaths of his wife and two children. These losses profoundly affected him and are reflected in some of his later compositions.

Requiem:

In addition to his operas, Verdi composed a famous Requiem Mass in memory of the Italian writer Alessandro Manzoni. The "Messa da Requiem" is a powerful and dramatic work that is often performed in concert settings.

Later Life:

Verdi's later years were marked by his retirement from opera composition, but he remained active in music and philanthropy. He donated generously to various causes and was involved in charitable work.

Legacy:

Giuseppe Verdi is considered one of the most important figures in the history of opera. His works continue to be performed worldwide, and he is celebrated for his contributions to the art form.

Death:

Verdi passed away on January 27, 1901, in Milan, Italy. His funeral was a national event, attended by thousands of people, and his legacy endures to this day.

Honors:

Verdi's contributions to Italian culture and music led to numerous honors and recognitions during his lifetime, including being named a Senator of the Kingdom of Italy.

Statue of Saint Francis of Paola

The Statue of Saint Francis of Paola is a religious monument in Palermo, Italy, dedicated to Saint Francis of Paola, a revered Christian saint known for his piety and asceticism. Here are some key details about this statue:

Location:

The Statue of Saint Francis of Paola can often be found in religious institutions, particularly in churches or chapels dedicated to the saint. There may be multiple statues or depictions of Saint Francis of Paola in various churches throughout Palermo.

Saint Francis of Paola:

Saint Francis of Paola (1416–1507) was an Italian mendicant friar and the founder of the Order of Minims. He is known for his austere and ascetic lifestyle, as well as his commitment to a life of poverty and humility. He performed numerous miracles during his lifetime and is venerated as a saint by the Catholic Church.

Monument Design:

The statue of Saint Francis of Paola typically portrays the saint in traditional religious attire, often with a long robe and a cross. His facial expression may convey a sense of serenity and piety.

Devotional Significance:

These statues serve as focal points for devotion and prayer among Catholics and those who have a special devotion to Saint Francis of Paola. Devotees may offer prayers or light candles in front of the statue as an expression of their faith and devotion.

Church Context:

Saint Francis of Paola is often associated with specific churches or religious institutions dedicated to him. His statues can be found within these places of worship, and they are often part of larger religious altars or displays.

Religious Festivals:

In some cases, statues of Saint Francis of Paola may play a prominent role in religious festivals or processions dedicated to the saint. These events often include the veneration of his relics or images.

Historical and Cultural Significance:

Saint Francis of Paola holds historical and cultural significance in the religious tradition of Palermo and beyond. His life and teachings continue to inspire and influence the faithful.

Bronze bust of Bernardino da Ucria

Bernardino da Ucria (1739-1796) was an Italian botanist, naturalist, and physician known for his contributions to the study of plants and animals in Sicily during the 18th century. He is often considered one of the pioneers of Sicilian botany and is particularly noted for his extensive work on the flora and fauna of the island. While Bernardino da Ucria may not be as widely recognized as some other historical figures, especially outside of the field of botany, there are several ways to learn more about him in Palermo:

Museo Regionale di Scienze Naturali (Regional Museum of Natural Sciences):

This museum in Palermo houses a significant collection of natural history specimens, including botanical specimens. It's possible that there may be exhibits or information related to Bernardino da Ucria's work and contributions within the museum.

Archives and Libraries:

Palermo has several historical archives and libraries that may contain documents, books, or manuscripts related to Bernardino da Ucria and his studies. These institutions may be able to provide more in-depth information about his life and work.

Botanical Gardens:

The Orto Botanico di Palermo (Botanical Garden of Palermo) is one of the oldest botanical gardens in Europe and played a significant role in Bernardino da Ucria's botanical research. A visit to the botanical garden may offer insights into the type of work he conducted.

Historical Sites:

While there may not be specific monuments or memorials dedicated to Bernardino da Ucria, his contributions to Sicilian natural history may be acknowledged or referenced in various historical and scientific contexts in Palermo.

CULTURAL TREASURES

In the heart of Sicily lies Palermo, a city that boasts an astonishing array of cultural treasures that span centuries and civilizations. From architectural marvels to artistic masterpieces, Palermo's cultural heritage is a testament to the richness of its history and the diversity of its influences. As you explore this captivating city, you'll be immersed in a tapestry of art, history, and expression that transcends time. Here, we delve into some of Palermo's most captivating cultural treasures that await you.

The Opera

Palermo boasts a rich opera tradition, and attending an opera performance here is an opportunity to immerse yourself in the grandeur of this art form while surrounded by historical beauty.

Teatro Massimo:

The Teatro Massimo is the heart of Palermo's opera scene and is renowned as one of the largest opera houses in Europe. This architectural masterpiece offers a grand setting for opera performances, combining spectacular acoustics with opulent décor. Its history and architecture alone make it a must-visit attraction, even if you're not attending a performance.

Selecting a Performance:

The Teatro Massimo hosts a variety of opera productions, ranging from classics by composers like Verdi and Puccini to contemporary works. Research the opera schedule in advance to select a performance that suits your preferences and schedule.

Booking Tickets:

Tickets for opera performances at Teatro Massimo can be purchased online, at the theater's box office, or through various ticket agencies. Consider booking tickets well in advance, especially for popular performances, to secure your preferred seating.

Dress Code:

Opera performances at Teatro Massimo often provide an opportunity to dress up elegantly. While there's no strict dress code, many attendees choose to wear smart or semi-formal attire to enhance the sense of occasion.

Arrival and Pre-Performance:

Arrive at the theater early to fully appreciate its grandeur and take in the pre-performance atmosphere. You can enjoy a drink or light meal at the theater's bar or nearby cafes before the show.

The Performance:

Opera performances at Teatro Massimo are a feast for the senses. As the orchestra tunes, the curtain rises, and the performers bring the story to life, you'll be transported by the power of music, singing, and storytelling.

Cultural and Emotional Experience:

Attending an opera performance in Palermo is not just about the music; it's a cultural and emotional experience. You'll witness the dedication of talented artists, the emotions conveyed through their performances, and the timeless stories that continue to resonate with audiences.

Baroque Architecture

Palermo's architectural landscape is graced by the opulent and ornate beauty of the Baroque style, a period marked by grandeur, drama, and artistic exuberance. As you stroll through the city's streets, you'll be transported back in time to an era of architectural innovation and expression.

Quattro Canti:

Begin your exploration with Quattro Canti, also known as Piazza Vigliena, a masterpiece that epitomizes Baroque urban planning. This octagonal intersection features four grand facades, each adorned with statues, fountains, and intricate decorations that pay homage to the Spanish Habsburg dynasty.

Teatro Massimo:

Make your way to the Teatro Massimo, one of Palermo's most iconic landmarks. This grand opera house showcases not only a dedication to the arts but also the opulence of the Baroque style, with lavish interiors, intricate ornamentation, and a breathtaking auditorium that promises an unforgettable cultural experience.

Oratorio di San Lorenzo:

Explore the Baroque masterpiece of Oratorio di San Lorenzo. This unassuming facade belies the exquisite interior, adorned with stucco decorations and frescoes that narrate the life of St. Lawrence. It's a testament to the hidden treasures that Palermo's Baroque architecture holds.

Chiesa di Santa Caterina:

Step inside the Chiesa di Santa Caterina, where you'll be enveloped by the artistic splendor of Baroque design. The nave's exuberant decoration, combined with the ornate side chapels, creates a captivating visual tapestry that reflects the period's affinity for lavish ornamentation.

Palazzo dei Normanni:

Visit the Palazzo dei Normanni, an architectural marvel that houses a blend of styles, including Norman, Arab, and Baroque. The Cappella Palatina within the palace showcases intricate mosaics and ornate stucco work that exemplify the opulence of the era.

Chiesa del Gesù:

Explore the Chiesa del Gesù, where the Baroque style is celebrated in its intricate details. The church's facade is adorned with elaborate carvings, and its interior features ornate altars, gilded decorations, and a sense of theatricality that defines the period.

Casa Professa:

Venture to Casa Professa, a Jesuit church that embodies the theatricality of the Baroque style. The church's facade boasts dynamic forms and sculptures, while its interiors reveal a harmonious interplay of light, color, and sculptural elements that create a spiritual and emotional impact.

Piazza Pretoria:

Stroll to Piazza Pretoria, where the Fontana Pretoria reigns as a sculptural masterpiece. This monumental fountain, adorned with mythological figures, embodies the spirit of Baroque excess, inviting contemplation and admiration.

Arab-Norman Architecture

Palermo, a city that stands at the crossroads of history and cultures, boasts a remarkable architectural legacy born from the harmonious fusion of Arab and Norman influences. This unique architectural style, prevalent in the 9th to 12th centuries, is a testament to the rich tapestry of interactions between civilizations. As you step into Palermo's streets in 2023 and beyond, you'll be transported back in time to witness the captivating embrace of Arab-Norman architecture, where elegance, diversity, and innovation converge.

A Lyrical Dialogue of Styles

The Arab-Norman architectural style is a poetic conversation between two distinct cultures. Arab design elements, characterized by intricate geometric patterns, ornate stucco work, and horseshoe arches, intertwine seamlessly with the solid lines and robust forms of Norman architecture. This synthesis creates a visual harmony that transcends cultural boundaries and tells the story of peaceful coexistence.

Monuments of Cultural Convergence

- **Cappella Palatina:** This chapel within the Norman Palace is a masterful embodiment of Arab-Norman architecture. Its intricate mosaics, rich with Byzantine, Arab, and Norman influences, portray religious and historical narratives, offering a visual testament to the interconnectedness of cultures.

- **Cattedrale di Palermo:** The Palermo Cathedral is a stunning example of the Arab-Norman style's grandeur. Its fusion of Romanesque, Gothic, and Arab motifs reflects the city's diverse heritage. The influence of Arab design is particularly evident in its main entrance and distinctive red domes.

- **Zisa and Cuba:** The Zisa and Cuba are two exemplary residences that showcase the marriage of Arab aesthetics and Norman solidity. The Zisa's intricate stucco designs and ornamental details echo Arab palatial architecture, while the Cuba's cubic form and fortress-like appearance reveal Norman influences.

Legacy in Details and Design

Beyond grand monuments, Palermo's Arab-Norman architecture is imprinted on the city's streets and structures, bearing witness to a heritage of artistic exchange. Horseshoe arches, intricately patterned ceramics, and geometric motifs can be found in various corners of the city, serving as a reminder of a time when diverse cultures converged and left an indelible mark on the urban landscape.

Cultural Continuity and Exploration

The legacy of Arab-Norman architecture in Palermo goes beyond physical structures; it's a cultural continuum that shapes the city's identity. While wandering through its streets, you'll feel the echoes of a bygone era and witness how the confluence of cultures has enriched Palermo's way of life.

Artistic Expressions

Palermo, a city that has long been a cultural crossroads, is a canvas adorned with a rich tapestry of artistic expressions. From ancient sculptures to contemporary installations, the city's artistic heritage paints a vivid picture of its history, diversity, and creativity. As you step into Palermo's artistic landscape in 2023 and beyond, prepare to be immersed in a world where every street, museum, and gallery tells a story through color, form, and imagination.

Sculptures

Sculptures grace Palermo's public spaces, capturing fleeting moments and eternalizing them in stone. The Fontana Pretoria, an elaborate fountain, stands as a Baroque masterpiece adorned with mythological figures and creatures, a testament to the city's artistic exuberance. The Genius of Palermo, a bronze sculpture symbolizing the city's spirit, offers an insight into modern sculptural expression.

Galleria d'Arte Moderna:

This gallery houses a collection of 19th and 20th-century artworks, reflecting Italy's evolution in the visual arts. From the dramatic chiaroscuro of Caravaggio to the innovative visions of contemporary artists, the gallery invites visitors to witness the progression of artistic thought and technique.

Street Art: Urban Narratives

Palermo's artistic expressions extend beyond traditional galleries, often making their mark on its streets and alleys. Street art serves as an alternative canvas for artists to express themselves, addressing social issues, cultural identity, and personal experiences. Murals and graffiti tell stories that resonate with the city's pulse, creating a dynamic and ever-changing urban gallery.

Music and Performing Arts: Symphony of Emotions

Palermo's artistic panorama is incomplete without its vibrant music and performing arts scene. Teatro Massimo, renowned for its opera performances, is a monument to the city's love for music and drama. The streets come alive with buskers and musicians, each note echoing the city's melodic spirit.

Palermo's Spirit in Art

Palermo's artistic expressions are more than mere works of art; they embody the city's soul, history, and aspirations. The amalgamation of artistic influences, from Norman and Arab architecture to contemporary street art, reveals the city's resilience and adaptability throughout the ages.

Embracing Art's Diversity

As you traverse Palermo's artistic landscape, embrace the diversity of forms, styles, and mediums that come together to shape the city's narrative. Engage with local artists, explore hidden galleries, and let your senses be heightened by the interplay of colors, textures, and ideas.

NATURE ADVENTURES

Beyond its rich cultural heritage, Palermo offers a gateway to nature's wonders—a chance to immerse yourself in the breathtaking landscapes, lush gardens, and serene escapes that adorn the city and its surroundings. In 2023 and beyond, as you venture into Palermo's natural realm, you're embarking on a journey that harmoniously complements the city's urban vibrancy with the tranquil beauty of the outdoors.

Mountain Hikes in Palermo

While Palermo is renowned for its cultural riches, it also offers an escape to nature's heights—a chance to embrace the serenity of the mountains and revel in the panoramic vistas they offer. In 2023 and beyond, as you embark on mountain hikes around Palermo, you're embarking on a journey that takes you closer to the skies, unveiling the city's surroundings from elevated perspectives.

Monte Pellegrino:

Monte Pellegrino stands as a beacon for mountain enthusiasts. Its rugged trails invite you to ascend its heights and be rewarded with unparalleled views of Palermo's coastline, the azure waters of the Mediterranean, and the city's urban tapestry sprawling below. As you hike through its trails, you're not just conquering a mountain; you're attaining a new perspective on Palermo's beauty.

Monte Gallo:

Monte Gallo offers another mountainous adventure, where your hike leads you to discover coastal panoramas that leave you breathless. From its summit, you'll gaze upon the sweeping sea, the Capo Gallo Nature Reserve, and the city that nestles against the shoreline—a harmonious blend of nature and civilization.

Pizzo Cane:

Pizzo Cane presents an opportunity for a more tranquil mountain experience. As you hike its trails, you'll find yourself immersed in a world of solitude, where the whispers of the wind and the rustle of vegetation accompany your journey. The summit provides a vantage point to admire the city's outskirts and the tranquil expanse beyond.

Exploring the Unknown:

Beyond these renowned peaks, Palermo's surrounding mountains offer a myriad of trails and routes waiting to be explored. Each path leads you through varying landscapes, from lush valleys to rocky terrains, and each ascent promises the satisfaction of reaching new heights and embracing the allure of the unknown.

Beaches and Coastal Beauty in Palermo

Palermo's allure extends beyond its historic charm and cultural riches—it embraces the coastline with a symphony of beaches and coastal vistas that invite you to unwind, explore, and connect with the Mediterranean's timeless beauty. In 2023 and beyond, as you venture to Palermo's shores, you're immersing yourself in a world where the city's energy converges with the tranquility of the sea.

Addaura Beach:

Addaura Beach offers a blend of history and relaxation. Nestled between rocky cliffs, this beach is known for its prehistoric cave dwellings—a testament to humanity's connection with this coastline throughout the ages. As you bask in the sun's glow, you're sharing the same shores that countless generations have enjoyed.

Isola delle Femmine:

Isola delle Femmine presents a tranquil escape from the urban rhythms. With its serene waters and rocky landscapes, it's a haven for those seeking solitude and natural beauty. Whether you're swimming, snorkeling, or simply strolling along the coast, this peaceful retreat invites you to embrace the simple pleasures of the sea.

Sferracavallo:

The village of Sferracavallo combines coastal charm with authentic local life. Its beaches, nestled between cliffs and coves, offer a quieter retreat where you can experience the authenticity of a fishing community. Indulge in seafood delicacies, explore the rugged coastline, and relish in the genuine warmth of the locals.

Mondello Beach:

Mondello Beach stands as a beacon of coastal beauty—a golden crescent adorned with fine sands and crystal-clear waters. Here, you can soak up the sun's warmth, cool off in the gentle waves, or indulge in water sports that invite adventure. The blend of natural splendor and vibrant local life creates an inviting atmosphere that resonates with both residents and visitors.

Gardens and Oases in Palermo

Amid the urban tapestry of Palermo, pockets of natural beauty and tranquility await in the form of gardens and oases. These serene havens offer a retreat from the bustling streets, inviting you to immerse yourself in lush landscapes, vibrant flora, and the soothing melodies of nature. In 2023 and beyond, as you explore Palermo's gardens, you're embarking on a journey where the city's energy converges with the serenity of green sanctuaries.

Orto Botanico di Palermo:

The Orto Botanico di Palermo is a testament to the city's dedication to preserving natural diversity. Within its boundaries, you'll find a symphony of plants from around the world, grouped in diverse themed gardens. Stroll through Mediterranean flora, admire succulent collections, and immerse yourself in a realm where colors, scents, and textures blend in harmonious unity.

Villa Giulia:

Villa Giulia offers a glimpse into Palermo's historical elegance. Amid its manicured gardens and ornate fountains, you can revel in the ambiance of a bygone era. As you explore the pathways lined with centuries-old trees, you're tracing the footsteps of nobility and discovering a respite that's both serene and regal.

Villa Bonanno:

Villa Bonanno, an urban oasis, provides a green sanctuary in the heart of the city. Here, you can find shade beneath towering trees, enjoy a leisurely stroll along its paths, and embrace a sense of calm that's a welcome contrast to the urban rhythms that surround it.

Villa Trabia:

Villa Trabia offers a romantic escape that transports you to a different time. With its charming layout, blooming gardens, and artistic statues, it's a testament to the city's appreciation for aesthetics and nature's beauty. The villa's allure lies in its ability to whisk you away from the present and envelop you in a world of enchantment.

Nature Reserves in Palermo

Amid the bustling cityscape of Palermo, nature reserves stand as sanctuaries of untamed beauty and ecological diversity. These protected areas offer a refuge for wildlife, a haven for biodiversity, and a space for visitors to connect with the raw splendor of the natural world. In 2023 and beyond, as you venture into Palermo's nature reserves, you're embarking on a journey that immerses you in landscapes that have been preserved in their unspoiled glory.

Capo Gallo Nature Reserve:

Capo Gallo Nature Reserve is a coastal gem that showcases the dynamic meeting of land and sea. With its rugged cliffs, azure waters, and diverse marine life, the reserve invites you to explore its trails, gaze upon breathtaking vistas, and perhaps even partake in snorkeling or diving to discover the underwater wonders that flourish along its shores.

Riserva Naturale dello Zingaro:

The Riserva Naturale dello Zingaro presents a pristine wilderness where untouched beauty reigns supreme. Its rocky coastline, hidden coves, and crystal-clear waters provide a backdrop for hiking trails that lead you through landscapes that feel untouched by time. Here, you're embraced by a sense of seclusion and a deep connection to nature.

Parco della Favorita:

Parco della Favorita offers a different kind of nature escape—a parkland that combines the allure of green spaces with historical significance. Originally created as a royal hunting ground, the park's expansive grounds feature trees, lawns, and avenues that lead to the majestic Palazzina Cinese—a testament to Palermo's connection with both nature and history.

National Parks in Palermo

Palermo's natural beauty extends beyond its urban confines, inviting you to discover the magnificence of its national parks—pristine landscapes that showcase the raw splendor of the island's diverse ecosystems. In 2023 and beyond, as you venture into Palermo's national parks, you're embarking on a journey that immerses you in some of Sicily's most breathtaking and untouched environments.

Parco delle Madonie:

Parco delle Madonie presents a captivating blend of rugged mountains, lush forests, and quaint villages. As you traverse its trails, you'll be enchanted by the diversity of plant and animal life that call these peaks and valleys home. The park's serene beauty and its harmonious coexistence with local communities reflect Palermo's commitment to conservation and sustainable living.

Parco Naturale Regionale delle Saline di Trapani e Paceco:

The Parco Naturale Regionale delle Saline di Trapani e Paceco is a unique treasure that embraces the interplay between human activity and nature's rhythms. Here, salt flats and ancient windmills provide a backdrop to vibrant wetlands—a habitat for migratory birds and delicate ecosystems. The park's significance extends beyond its environmental value; it's a cultural landscape that reflects Palermo's historical connection with the land.

Wildlife in Palermo

Beyond its historical and cultural riches, Palermo is a gateway to a diverse array of wildlife that calls the island of Sicily home. From the Mediterranean Sea to the mountain ranges, the city's surroundings are teeming with life, offering a glimpse into the natural tapestry that enriches the region. In 2023 and beyond, as you explore Palermo's wildlife, you're embarking on a journey that unveils the intricate connections between species and their habitats.

Marine Wonders of the Mediterranean

The Mediterranean Sea that graces Palermo's shores is a treasure trove of marine life. As you venture into its waters, you might encounter dolphins playfully dancing in the waves or sea turtles gliding gracefully beneath the surface. The sea's biodiversity is a testament to its role as a nurturing environment for a wide range of species.

Avian Spectacles

Palermo's skies are alive with the songs and flights of various bird species. From the majestic sight of migratory birds filling the air during seasonal migrations to the graceful presence of seagulls along the coast, the avian residents of Palermo's landscapes are an integral part of its natural beauty.

Mountain and Forest Residents

In the mountainous regions surrounding Palermo, you'll find a variety of mammals and fauna that have adapted to these rugged landscapes. Foxes, wild boars, and other small mammals call the hills and forests home, while rare plant species add vibrant splashes of color to the terrain.

BEST ACTIVITIES

Embark on a series of thrilling outdoor adventures in and around Palermo, where the beauty of nature becomes your playground. From scenic hikes to exhilarating water activities, this collection of outdoor experiences allows you to immerse yourself in Sicily's stunning landscapes and explore the region's natural wonders.

Mountain Biking in the Madonie Mountains

Gear up for a mountain biking excursion in the Madonie Mountains, a picturesque range characterized by rolling hills, dense forests, and charming villages. Traverse scenic trails that cater to various skill levels, offering both adrenaline-pumping descents and tranquil stretches.

Hiking in the Zingaro Nature Reserve

Begin your outdoor adventure with a hike in the Zingaro Nature Reserve, a pristine coastal area renowned for its rugged cliffs, crystal-clear waters, and diverse flora and fauna. Follow scenic trails that lead you to hidden coves, panoramic viewpoints, and opportunities for wildlife spotting.

Rock Climbing at Monte Pellegrino

Challenge yourself with a rock climbing adventure at Monte Pellegrino, an iconic peak overlooking Palermo. Whether you're a novice or an experienced climber, the rugged cliffs and breathtaking vistas provide an exhilarating backdrop for your ascent.

Kayaking along Sicily's Coastline

Embark on a kayaking journey along Sicily's pristine coastline, paddling through azure waters and exploring hidden sea caves. Marvel at the dramatic cliffs, and take in the tranquility as you navigate the waves and discover secluded coves.

Snorkeling and Diving in Isola delle Femmine

Dive into the vibrant underwater world of Isola delle Femmine, a marine protected area teeming with marine life and colorful corals. Whether you're snorkeling near the surface or exploring deeper depths through scuba diving, you'll be treated to an unforgettable aquatic adventure.

Countryside Horseback Riding

Saddle up for a horseback riding experience through Palermo's picturesque countryside. Trot along scenic trails, passing through olive groves, vineyards, and charming rural landscapes, all while enjoying a unique perspective of the region.

Sailing in the Tyrrhenian Sea

Set sail in the Tyrrhenian Sea for a sailing adventure that allows you to experience Palermo's coastline from a different angle. Feel the wind in your hair as you glide across the water, stopping at tranquil bays for swimming and relaxation.

Camping under the Sicilian Sky

Embrace the great outdoors with a camping excursion in Sicily's scenic locations. Whether you choose to camp near the beach, in the mountains, or in the countryside, you'll be treated to stunning sunsets, stargazing, and the simple joys of connecting with nature.

Water activities

Palermo, situated on the beautiful island of Sicily, offers a variety of water-related activities due to its proximity to the Mediterranean Sea and its rich coastline. Here are some water activities you can enjoy in and around Palermo:

Beach Relaxation:

Palermo boasts several beautiful beaches along its coastline, including Mondello Beach and Aspra Beach. Relax on the sandy shores, swim in the clear waters, and soak up the Mediterranean sun.

Swimming and Snorkeling:

The Mediterranean waters around Palermo are great for swimming, and some areas offer excellent snorkeling opportunities. Explore the underwater world and observe marine life in its natural habitat.

Waterfront Promenades:

Stroll along Palermo's scenic waterfront promenades, such as Foro Italico and the Promenade of the Marina. These areas are perfect for leisurely walks and enjoying sea views.

Scuba Diving:

There are scuba diving centers in Palermo that offer diving courses and guided dives for divers of all skill levels. Explore underwater caves, shipwrecks, and vibrant marine ecosystems.

Boat Tours:

Take a boat tour along the coast to admire Palermo's picturesque landscapes and historical sites from the sea. Sunset cruises and dolphin-watching tours are also popular options.

Sailing:

Rent a sailboat or join a sailing excursion to experience the joys of sailing in the Mediterranean. Palermo's coastline provides great sailing conditions and stunning views.

Jet Skiing:

Rent a jet ski and have an adrenaline-packed adventure along the coast. Some beach areas offer jet ski rentals for visitors.

Windsurfing and Kitesurfing:

The area around Palermo is known for its winds, making it suitable for windsurfing and kitesurfing. There are schools and rental centers for those interested in trying these water sports.

Canoeing and Kayaking:

Paddle along the coast or explore the natural reserves and lagoons near Palermo by canoe or kayak. This is a peaceful way to enjoy the region's natural beauty.

Stand-Up Paddleboarding (SUP):

Try stand-up paddleboarding along the calm waters of the Mediterranean. Many beaches offer SUP rentals, and it's an enjoyable way to stay active on the water.

Waterfront Dining:

Enjoy fresh seafood and Mediterranean cuisine at waterfront restaurants and cafés. Many dining establishments in Palermo offer picturesque views of the sea.

Fishing:

Join a fishing excursion to experience traditional Sicilian fishing techniques and enjoy the thrill of catching your own seafood. It's a great way to connect with local culture and cuisine.

Breathtaking Sunset spots

Palermo, with its stunning Mediterranean coastline and historical architecture, offers several beautiful spots to enjoy breathtaking sunsets. Here are some of the best sunset spots in and around Palermo:

Mondello Beach:

The beach at Mondello is a fantastic place to watch the sunset. As the sun dips below the horizon, it casts a warm glow on the picturesque bay and the Art Nouveau architecture that lines the waterfront.

Monte Pellegrino:

This mountain, located just outside Palermo, offers panoramic views of the city and the sea. The sunset from Monte Pellegrino is particularly stunning, and there's a sanctuary at the summit where you can enjoy the view.

Foro Italico:

The waterfront promenade of Foro Italico is a popular spot to watch the sunset. You can take a leisurely stroll along the seafront while the sun paints the sky with vivid colors.

Teatro Massimo:

The steps of Teatro Massimo, the grand opera house of Palermo, provide a unique perspective for viewing the sunset. Enjoy the contrast of the historic theater against the setting sun.

Quattro Canti:

This Baroque square in the heart of Palermo features four corners adorned with statues and architectural details. It's a central point to watch the sun's warm glow on the historic buildings.

Castello della Zisa:

Located within the Zisa Park, this historic castle offers a peaceful setting to enjoy the sunset. The combination of the castle's architecture and the setting sun creates a magical ambiance.

La Cala:

The old port of Palermo, known as La Cala, is a charming area to watch the sunset. It's a tranquil spot where you can take in the views of boats and the sea against the evening sky.

Vucciria Market Rooftop Bars:

Some rooftop bars in the Vucciria area offer great sunset views over the city. It's a perfect spot to relax with a drink and enjoy the transition from day to night.

Cefalù:

While not in Palermo, the coastal town of Cefalù, about an hour's drive from Palermo, offers some of the most stunning sunset views in Sicily. The town's beach and medieval architecture make for a picturesque backdrop.

Boat Tours:

Consider taking a sunset boat tour along the coast. This provides a unique perspective and the opportunity to see the sunset from the water.

LOCAL FOOD MARKETS AND STREET LIFE

Palermo's pulse beats in its bustling streets and lively markets, where the city's vibrant spirit comes to life. As you step into Palermo's streets in 2023 and beyond, prepare to be swept away by the vivacious energy, colorful chaos, and authentic experiences that define its local markets and street life. This is where the essence of the city truly reveals itself—a tapestry of culture, flavors, and human connections.

Vibrant Markets

Step into Palermo's vibrant markets, and you'll find yourself enveloped in a sensory feast that transports you to the heart of Sicilian culture. These bustling marketplaces, alive with colors, aromas, and the lively chatter of vendors, embody the very essence of the city's spirit. In 2023 and beyond, immerse yourself in the lively symphony of Palermo's markets, where every corner is a treasure trove waiting to be discovered, and every moment is an invitation to indulge your senses.

Mercato di Ballarò:

Wander through the lively alleys of Ballarò Market, where a kaleidoscope of colors unfolds before your eyes. Vibrant fruits, aromatic herbs, and the freshest seafood create an artistic tapestry that pays homage to the bounties of Sicilian land and sea.

Mercato di Vucciria:

In the heart of the historic district, Vucciria Market exudes an authentic atmosphere that harks back to Palermo's storied past. The riot of colors from hanging spices, stacks of vegetables, and vibrant textiles intermingles with the sounds of banter and the clinking of glasses.

Street Food Extravaganza

Palermo's markets are also a gastronomic playground, where street food reigns supreme. Sample the iconic arancini, their golden exteriors hiding delectable surprises within. Savor the unmistakable aroma of pane con panelle, as chickpea fritters are wedged into soft bread, creating a symphony of textures and flavors.

Engaging with Local Life

More than just a shopping experience, Palermo's markets offer an opportunity to connect with locals and delve into their way of life. Engage in friendly conversations with vendors, who are eager to share their stories, culinary tips, and insights into the city's history and culture.

Capturing Authentic Moments

In Palermo's markets, every moment is a snapshot of authenticity. Watch as artisans skillfully craft intricate ceramics or butchers skillfully prepare their cuts of meat. Capture the essence of daily life as shoppers carefully select the ripest fruits and the freshest catches.

Street Food

In the charming city of Palermo, the streets come alive not just with vibrant culture, but also with an array of delectable street food that reflects the heart and soul of Sicilian cuisine. As you explore the bustling streets in 2023 and beyond, prepare to embark on a tantalizing gastronomic journey, where every bite tells a story of tradition, history, and the irresistible flavors that define Palermo's street food scene.

Arancini:

At the heart of Palermo's street food culture are the beloved arancini, delightful golden-brown rice balls that come stuffed with a variety of fillings. From classic ragù (meat sauce) and mozzarella to spinach and cheese, each arancino is a bite-sized treasure bursting with flavor. These savory delights offer a perfect balance of textures and a taste that embodies the essence of Sicily.

Pane con Panelle:

For an authentic taste of Sicilian heritage, indulge in a pane con panelle. This simple yet incredibly satisfying treat consists of chickpea fritters sandwiched between soft bread. The contrast between the crispy panelle and the pillowy bread creates a harmonious symphony of flavors and textures that captures the spirit of Palermo's street cuisine.

Crocchè:

Another street food staple in Palermo is the crocchè, a potato croquette that's crispy on the outside and wonderfully creamy on the inside. Seasoned with herbs and spices, these golden bites are both a comforting snack and a tribute to the city's culinary creativity.

Cannoli:

While Palermo's street food scene is often associated with savory treats, it wouldn't be complete without a touch of sweetness. Sink your teeth into a classic Sicilian dessert, the cannolo, a tube-shaped pastry filled with sweet ricotta cheese and often adorned with candied fruit or chocolate chips. The combination of creamy filling and crispy shell is an irresistible match made in culinary heaven.

Caponata:

Caponata embodies Palermo's love affair with vegetables. This sweet and sour dish features a medley of eggplant, peppers, tomatoes, and olives, often cooked with a touch of vinegar and sugar. The result is a harmonious blend of flavors that celebrates the region's abundant produce.

Pasta con le Sarde:

Pasta con le Sarde offers a taste of the sea that's deeply intertwined with Palermo's history. This pasta dish combines sardines with fennel, raisins, and pine nuts—a combination that reflects the city's connection to Arab influences and its ability to infuse unique flavors into traditional recipes.

Cassata:

For dessert, Cassata takes the spotlight—a sweet masterpiece that embodies Palermo's artistry in the kitchen. Layers of sponge cake are filled with ricotta cheese, candied fruits, and marzipan, creating a dessert that's both rich and delicate. The vibrant colors and intricate decorations make it a visual delight as well as a culinary experience.

Sfincione:

Sfincione, often referred to as Sicilian pizza, showcases the city's unique take on this beloved dish. With its thick, fluffy crust topped with a medley of ingredients like tomatoes, onions, and anchovies, sfincione is a hearty and flavorful treat that's perfect for a quick snack on the go.

Pane con la Milza:

Pane con la Milza is a culinary experience that captures Palermo's bold flavors. This sandwich features tender slices of veal spleen sautéed with lard, cheese, and a sprinkle of lemon juice, all enclosed in a rustic roll. It's a dish that's not only a delicious indulgence but also a reflection of Palermo's unique culinary identity.

Ballarò Market

Nestled within the heart of Palermo, Ballarò Market stands as a testament to the city's vibrant spirit and diverse cultural heritage. As you step into this bustling market in 2023 and beyond, you'll be transported to a world of vibrant colors, fragrant aromas, and the lively symphony of vendors and shoppers. Ballarò Market isn't just a place to shop; it's a sensory journey that offers a glimpse into the soul of Palermo's culinary and cultural identity.

A Kaleidoscope of Colors and Flavors

Ballarò Market is a visual feast, where every corner reveals a dazzling display of colors. From the vibrant fruits and vegetables to the array of spices and herbs, the market's vibrant palette reflects the richness of Sicilian produce. The sight of fresh seafood glistening on ice and the stacks of olives and cheeses are a testament to the market's role as a hub of culinary exploration.

Culinary Delights and Sicilian Specialties

Explore the maze-like alleys of Ballarò Market and you'll uncover a treasure trove of culinary delights. Savor the intoxicating aroma of freshly baked bread and pastries that beckon you to artisanal bakeries. Discover local cheeses, cured meats, and olives that capture the essence of Sicilian gastronomy. And of course, don't miss the chance to indulge in iconic street food such as arancini and panelle.

Cultural Fusion and Authentic Encounters

Ballarò Market is a microcosm of Palermo's diverse cultural history. Here, Arab, Norman, and other influences converge in a harmonious blend that's reflected in the array of products and the interactions between vendors and visitors. Engage in conversations with the passionate vendors, many of whom have been part of the market's fabric for generations. Their stories and insights offer a unique glimpse into the city's history and traditions.

Hidden Gems and Treasures

Beyond the stalls of produce and food, Ballarò Market also reveals hidden gems. Antique shops, local crafts, and even small art galleries can be found in the vicinity, adding an extra layer of cultural exploration to your visit. These tucked-away spots offer a glimpse into the creative pulse of the city.

Capo Market

Nestled within the heart of Palermo, the Capo Market invites you to embark on a sensory journey that's as much a feast for the eyes as it is for the palate. In 2023 and beyond, as you step into this lively market, you'll find yourself immersed in a kaleidoscope of colors, flavors, and the vibrant spirit that defines Palermo's cultural tapestry. Capo Market isn't just a place to shop—it's an exploration of Sicilian traditions, culinary wonders, and the timeless art of human interaction.

A Symphony of Colors and Aromas

Capo Market is a symphony of vibrant hues and tantalizing aromas that converge to create an immersive experience. As you stroll through its lively alleys, you'll be captivated by the sight of plump fruits, fragrant herbs, and fresh seafood that seem to sing the songs of the sea. The market's bustling ambiance is complemented by the joyful banter of vendors, creating an atmosphere that's alive with energy and excitement.

Culinary Adventures and Sicilian Treasures

From fresh produce to local specialties, Capo Market offers a captivating array of culinary treasures. Engage with vendors who are passionate about their products, and let their recommendations guide your culinary journey. Discover the rich flavors of cheeses, olives, cured meats, and other iconic Sicilian ingredients that are a testament to the region's gastronomic excellence.

Traditional Delights and Street Food

Capo Market is a haven for those seeking authentic Sicilian street food experiences. Indulge in the iconic arancini, whose golden exteriors give way to flavorful fillings. Savor the crispy delights of crocchè, and be sure to experience the rich sweetness of cannoli, a beloved Sicilian dessert that's a symphony of creamy ricotta and crispy pastry.

Cultural Interactions and Local Insights

One of the most rewarding aspects of visiting Capo Market is the opportunity to interact with the vendors and soak in the local culture. Strike up conversations, ask questions, and immerse yourself in the stories that vendors are often eager to share. These exchanges provide a window into the city's history, traditions, and the warm hospitality that characterizes Palermo.

Hidden Gems and Artistic Touches

Beyond the culinary delights, Capo Market holds surprises at every corner. Discover small artisan shops, selling traditional crafts and souvenirs that embody the city's artistic spirit. The intricate ceramics and unique finds add an extra layer of authenticity to your experience.

PALERMO TOURS

Here are diverse tour options that will allow you to explore and experience the beauty, history, culture, and flavors of Palermo.

Historical Walking Tour

Embark on a captivating journey through Palermo's rich history with a walking tour that takes you on a chronological exploration of the city's most significant landmarks, revealing layers of stories and cultural influences along the way.

Meeting Point: Quattro Canti

Your historical walking tour begins at Quattro Canti, the heart of Baroque Palermo. As you stand at this octagonal intersection, your guide sets the stage for the tour, introducing you to the city's history and the importance of this iconic square.

Palermo Cathedral: A Window to the Ages

From Quattro Canti, follow your guide to Palermo Cathedral, a masterpiece that showcases an amalgamation of architectural styles. As you admire the Norman-Arab-Byzantine design, learn about its historical transformations and its role as a symbol of the city's diverse cultural heritage.

Chiesa del Gesù: A Baroque Marvel

Your tour continues to the Chiesa del Gesù, where you'll immerse yourself in the opulence of Baroque architecture. Stand in awe of the intricate facade and step inside to marvel at the vibrant interiors adorned with gilded details, cherubs, and ornate altars.

Piazza Pretoria: A Fountain of Stories

As you navigate through Palermo's streets, arrive at Piazza Pretoria. Here, the Fontana Pretoria commands attention, its sculptural figures telling tales of mythology and history. Your guide unravels the stories behind the fountain's creation and its significance in the city's past.

Casa Professa: A Sanctuary of Artistry

A short walk leads you to Casa Professa, a Jesuit church that's an embodiment of the Baroque style. Marvel at the intricate facade and venture inside to experience the harmonious interplay of light, color, and sculptures that create an atmosphere of devotion and artistic brilliance.

Piazza Bellini: A Window into Arab Influence

Continuing your journey, you reach Piazza Bellini, home to La Martorana Church. Delve into the church's history, emphasizing its blend of Norman and Arab architectural elements. Inside, the Byzantine mosaics come to life, narrating tales of saints and spirituality.

Norman Palace and Palatine Chapel: A Royal Legacy

The tour takes you to the Norman Palace, an imposing fortress that witnessed centuries of rule. Explore its historical significance and enter the Palatine Chapel, where breathtaking mosaics fuse Byzantine and Norman artistry, reflecting the crossroads of cultures that shaped Palermo.

Oratorio di San Lorenzo: A Hidden Gem

Your journey concludes at the Oratorio di San Lorenzo, a hidden gem that encapsulates the essence of Palermo's history. The unassuming exterior gives way to an interior adorned with stucco decorations and frescoes that tell the story of St. Lawrence and the city's past.

Reflection and Appreciation

As you bid farewell to your guide, take a moment to reflect on the wealth of history and cultural diversity you've encountered during your historical walking tour. Palermo's streets have shared their stories with you, leaving you with a deeper understanding of the city's past and a greater appreciation for its enduring heritage.

Street Food Tour

Embark on an enticing journey through Palermo's bustling streets, where aromas and tastes mingle in a symphony of culinary delight. This street food tour is your ticket to savoring Palermo's authentic flavors, from savory snacks to sweet treats, as you explore the vibrant local food scene.

Meeting Point: Ballarò Market

Your street food adventure commences at the vibrant Ballarò Market, a lively hub of activity and a treasure trove of ingredients. Here, your guide introduces you to the sights, sounds, and aromas that define Palermo's street food culture.

Arancini Delights: The Sicilian Classic

Indulge in your first taste of Sicilian street food: arancini. These golden fried rice balls are filled with a variety of delicious fillings, from classic ragù to spinach and cheese. Savor the crisp exterior and the explosion of flavors within.

Pane e Panelle: A Chickpea Treat

Next, it's time to experience pane e panelle, a local favorite. Enjoy a freshly made chickpea fritter sandwiched between soft bread, showcasing the simple yet satisfying combination of textures and flavors.

Sicilian Sweets: Cannoli and Cassata

No street food tour in Palermo is complete without sampling iconic Sicilian sweets. Bite into a crispy cannolo, filled with sweet ricotta and adorned with candied fruit. Then, savor the intricate layers of cassata, a cake rich with marzipan, candied fruit, and a touch of citrus.

Pane ca' Meusa: A Palermo Tradition

Delve into the heart of Palermo's street food culture with pane ca' meusa—a sandwich filled with tender veal spleen cooked to perfection and topped with caciocavallo cheese. This dish offers a unique taste of local tradition.

Focaccia and More: Street Food Diversity

As you continue your tour, sample slices of focaccia adorned with a variety of toppings, from olives to tomatoes. Discover how diverse ingredients come together to create delightful and flavorful combinations.

Sfincione: Palermo's Pizza

Treat your taste buds to sfincione, a unique Palermo-style pizza. Savor the thick, fluffy dough topped with a tomato and onion sauce, as well as a sprinkling of breadcrumbs, cheese, and oregano.

Reflection and Culinary Memories

As your street food tour draws to a close, take a moment to reflect on the array of flavors, textures, and aromas that have delighted your senses. Palermo's street food is not just about taste—it's about culture, tradition, and the joy of sharing food with others.

Art and Architecture Tour

Embark on an enlightening journey through Palermo's artistic treasures and architectural marvels. This tour takes you on a captivating exploration of the city's diverse art forms, from historic landmarks to contemporary galleries, offering insights into its rich cultural tapestry.

Meeting Point: Teatro Massimo

Your art and architecture tour commences at the grand Teatro Massimo, an iconic opera house that seamlessly marries architectural splendor with artistic excellence. Here, your guide sets the stage for a journey that celebrates Palermo's creative legacy.

Chiesa del Gesù: Baroque Brilliance

Begin your exploration of Palermo's artistic heritage at the Chiesa del Gesù, a prime example of Baroque architecture. Marvel at the intricate facade adorned with sculptural details, and step inside to immerse yourself in the ornate interiors and lavish altars.

Quattro Canti: Urban Masterpiece

Stroll to Quattro Canti, where the symmetrical Baroque facades frame the intersection in a display of urban planning at its finest. Delve into the symbolism and history behind this architectural gem, appreciating its role as a testament to the city's historical and artistic heritage.

Palazzo dei Normanni: Architecture and History Blend

Your tour takes you to the Palazzo dei Normanni, a blend of architectural styles that tells the story of Palermo's evolution. Explore its diverse rooms, including the awe-inspiring Palatine Chapel adorned with intricate mosaics that narrate a visual tale of cultural encounters.

Galleria d'Arte Moderna: Contemporary Perspectives

Transition from historical to contemporary art at the Galleria d'Arte Moderna. Discover a collection of artworks that offer a window into Palermo's modern artistic expressions, showcasing the city's ongoing engagement with the creative spirit.

Orto Botanico: Nature and Artistry

Venture to the Orto Botanico, where the beauty of nature blends with artistic design. Admire the carefully curated plant collections and landscaping that create a living canvas of colors and textures.

Palazzo Abatellis: Renaissance Treasures

Experience the Renaissance influence at Palazzo Abatellis, home to a remarkable collection of art. Explore the museum's rich offerings, including paintings, sculptures, and decorative arts, all set within the exquisite halls of this historic palace.

Museo Salinas: Ancient Treasures

Your tour takes you to Museo Salinas, a place where ancient art and culture come alive. Marvel at the Greek and Roman sculptures that offer a glimpse into the past, underscoring Palermo's enduring connection to history.

Reflection and Artistic Reverie

As you conclude your tour, take a moment to reflect on the diverse artistic expressions that have unfolded before you. Palermo's art and architecture are not just markers of its past—they are a testament to its ongoing cultural vibrancy and creative spirit.

Nighttime Ghost Tour

Step into the enigmatic realm of Palermo's past as the sun sets and the city's streets come alive with whispered tales and lingering mysteries. This immersive ghost tour takes you on a journey through Palermo's haunted history, revealing eerie legends and spine-chilling stories that have woven themselves into its streets and buildings.

Meeting Point: Piazza Bellini

Your ghostly adventure begins in Piazza Bellini, a place that wears its layers of history like a shroud. As the night deepens, your guide sets the tone for a journey that will lead you through the city's darker corners.

Catacombs of the Capuchin Monastery: A Haunting Descent

Descend into the depths of the Catacombs of the Capuchin Monastery, a place where time seems suspended and whispers of the past linger in the air. As you explore these eerie chambers filled with mummified remains, your guide recounts the stories of those who rest here.

Quattro Canti: Ghosts of the Intersection

Stroll to Quattro Canti, where the grand facades are illuminated by the soft glow of streetlights. Learn about the lingering spirits and mysterious occurrences associated with this iconic intersection.

Palazzo dei Normanni: Haunting Histories

Your tour takes you to the Palazzo dei Normanni, a place that has witnessed centuries of power struggles and secrets. As you wander through its historic halls, your guide shares chilling stories that blur the line between the living and the supernatural.

Cappella Palatina: Spirits of the Chapel

Enter the Cappella Palatina, where the flickering candlelight casts shadows on the intricate mosaics. Listen to tales of apparitions and inexplicable occurrences that are said to have taken place within these sacred walls.

Chiesa del Carmine: Echoes of the Past

Visit the Chiesa del Carmine, where the darkness seems to conceal forgotten stories and echoes of the past. Learn about the mysterious events that have shaped the church's haunted reputation.

Street of the Spirits: Via dei Crociferi

Wander through Via dei Crociferi, a street that's said to be frequented by spirits. As you walk along its cobblestones, your guide reveals the ghostly encounters and unexplained phenomena that have left their mark on this atmospheric thoroughfare.

Piazza Pretoria: Legends of the Fountain

Arrive at Piazza Pretoria, where the Fontana Pretoria stands as a silent witness to the city's history. Hear tales of curses, tragedies, and the unsettling presence that some say lingers around the fountain.

Reflection and the Unseen

As your ghost tour draws to a close, pause for a moment to reflect on the stories you've heard and the hidden layers of Palermo's history that have been revealed. The city's past, both tangible and spectral, has been unveiled before your eyes.

Palermo Bike Tour

Discover Palermo in a unique and active way with a bike tour that takes you through its charming streets, historic sites, and vibrant neighborhoods. This guided journey on two wheels offers a dynamic perspective on the city's rich history, cultural diversity, and architectural splendor.

Meeting Point: Teatro Massimo

Your bike tour begins at the iconic Teatro Massimo, where your guide introduces you to the adventure that awaits. As you gear up and mount your bike, you'll feel the excitement building for the exploration ahead.

Quattro Canti: A Cycling Overture

Start your ride at Quattro Canti, the architectural masterpiece that serves as a crossroads of history and culture. Your guide shares insights into the symbolism and stories behind this captivating intersection.

Palazzo dei Normanni: Cycling through Royalty

Pedal to the Palazzo dei Normanni, an architectural gem that holds centuries of stories within its walls. As you cycle through its courtyards, you'll learn about its historical significance and the architectural influences that have shaped it.

Cattedrale di Palermo: Stories in Stone

Your bike tour continues to the Cattedrale di Palermo, an imposing structure that showcases a fusion of architectural styles. Park your bike and explore its intricate details, discovering the layers of history etched into its stone.

Chiesa del Gesù: Baroque Charms

Cycle to the Chiesa del Gesù, a Baroque masterpiece that exudes grandeur from every angle. Park your bike nearby and venture inside to experience the visual feast of sculptures, frescoes, and decorative details.

Piazza Pretoria: Cycling Through Legends

Arrive at Piazza Pretoria, where the Fontana Pretoria reigns as a sculptural marvel. Park your bike and explore the stories behind the fountain's creation, appreciating the intricate carvings that have tales to tell.

Orto Botanico: Nature on Wheels

Switch gears and pedal to the Orto Botanico, a serene oasis where nature and artistry intertwine. As you navigate the pathways, enjoy the lush greenery and the botanical wonders that surround you.

Kalsa District: Cycling through Creativity

Explore the Kalsa district, a creative hub that's home to art studios, galleries, and hidden courtyards. Cycle through its winding streets, immersing yourself in its bohemian atmosphere and artistic energy.

Capo Market: Cycling and Culinary Discovery

Ride to the Capo Market, where the aromas of fresh produce and local delicacies fill the air. Park your bike and explore the bustling stalls, indulging in a sensory feast of sights, smells, and flavors.

Reflection and Active Memories

As you conclude your bike tour, take a moment to reflect on the sights, sounds, and experiences that have enriched your journey. Palermo's streets have become pathways of discovery, and your bike tour has allowed you to engage with the city's history and culture in a dynamic and memorable way.

Segway Tour

Embark on a unique and effortless adventure through Palermo's historic streets and vibrant neighborhoods on a Segway tour. This guided journey offers an exciting way to explore the city's rich history, architectural marvels, and cultural treasures, all while experiencing the thrill of gliding on two wheels.

Meeting Point: Teatro Massimo

Your Segway tour begins at the iconic Teatro Massimo, where your guide introduces you to the Segway and provides a brief training session to ensure your comfort and safety. As you become familiar with the Segway's controls, the anticipation of the tour ahead builds.

Quattro Canti: A Segway Symphony

Glide through Quattro Canti, where the grand facades create an architectural ensemble that encapsulates the city's history and cultural influences. Your guide provides insights into the symbolism and stories that are woven into this unique intersection.

Palazzo dei Normanni: Royal Ride

Continue your Segway journey to the Palazzo dei Normanni, an imposing structure that has stood witness to centuries of history. Cruise through its courtyards and gardens, as your guide shares anecdotes about its royal past and architectural significance.

Cattedrale di Palermo: Effortless Exploration

Arrive at the Cattedrale di Palermo, an architectural masterpiece that reveals the city's diverse influences. As you seamlessly navigate around its exterior, your guide offers insights into the cathedral's intricate details and historical context.

Chiesa del Gesù: Baroque Elegance

Glide to the Chiesa del Gesù, a Baroque gem that exudes grandeur and elegance. Maneuver your Segway with ease as you approach the ornate facade, and pause to appreciate the sculptural and decorative elements that define its beauty.

Piazza Pretoria: Segway through Legends

Arrive at Piazza Pretoria, where the Fontana Pretoria stands as a silent witness to tales of history and myth. Explore the stories behind the fountain's creation, and take in the intricate carvings that adorn its sculptural figures.

Orto Botanico: Nature and Technology Merge

Transition from the streets to the serene Orto Botanico, gliding through its pathways surrounded by lush greenery and botanical wonders. The Segway effortlessly adapts to the changing terrain as you explore this oasis of nature and artistry.

Kalsa District: A Segway Adventure

Experience the charm of the Kalsa district, gliding through its artistic streets and discovering hidden courtyards. Your Segway effortlessly navigates the winding paths, allowing you to absorb the bohemian atmosphere and creative energy.

Capo Market: A Culinary Cruise

Navigate to the bustling Capo Market, where the sights and sounds of fresh produce and local delicacies fill the air.

Effortlessly navigate the market's stalls, savoring the sensory feast of colors, aromas, and flavors.

Reflection and Futuristic Memories

As your Segway tour comes to a close, take a moment to reflect on the experiences and sights that have unfolded during your adventure. Your Segway has been a futuristic vessel that has transported you through Palermo's history and culture, offering a unique and memorable perspective.

Mafia History Tour

Embark on a compelling and enlightening journey through Palermo's complex history with the Mafia. This tour delves deep into the city's past, revealing the rise, impact, and ongoing efforts to combat organized crime. As you explore significant sites, you'll gain insight into the intricate relationship between Palermo and the Mafia.

Meeting Point: Palermo Historical Center

Your Mafia history tour begins in the heart of Palermo, where your guide introduces you to the context and significance of this journey. Prepare to navigate the intertwining narratives of power, corruption, and societal transformation.

Piazza della Memoria: Honoring the Victims

Visit Piazza della Memoria, a poignant tribute to Mafia victims. Here, your guide shares stories of those who resisted the Mafia's influence and paid the ultimate price. Reflect on the resilience of individuals who stood against the criminal organization.

Addaura Caves: A Hidden History

Venture to the Addaura Caves, which served as secret meeting places for Mafia bosses in the past. As you explore these caves, your guide unravels the historical connections and the role they played in Mafia operations.

Uditore Park: The Falcone-Borsellino Monument

Pay your respects at the Falcone-Borsellino Monument in Uditore Park, commemorating two courageous judges who dedicated their lives to combating the Mafia. Learn about their legacy and the challenges they faced in their pursuit of justice.

Capaci: The Site of a Tragedy

Arrive at Capaci, where a haunting monument stands in memory of the Capaci bombing, a pivotal event in Mafia history. Listen to the accounts of the attack and its aftermath, marking a turning point in public perception and government action.

Maxi Trial Courthouse: A Defining Moment

Visit the courthouse where the Maxi Trial took place—a landmark case that saw hundreds of Mafia members put on trial. Explore the significance of this trial and the impact it had on dismantling organized crime networks.

Palermo Historical Sites: The Mafia's Influence

As you navigate through Palermo's streets, your guide points out historical sites that were once intertwined with the Mafia's operations. These locations provide context for understanding the organization's reach and its complex relationship with the city.

Anti-Mafia Organizations: Hope for Change

Learn about the efforts of anti-Mafia organizations and individuals who have worked tirelessly to combat organized crime. Discover how their initiatives have brought about social change, community empowerment, and a renewed sense of hope.

Reflection and Societal Progress

As your Mafia history tour comes to a close, take a moment to reflect on the stories you've heard and the impact of organized crime on Palermo's past and present. Consider the strides that have been made in confronting this challenge and the ongoing commitment to creating a more just and resilient society.

Wine Tasting Tour

Indulge in a sensory journey through Palermo's wine culture with a wine tasting tour that takes you to the heart of Sicilian terroir. This guided exploration introduces you to the region's diverse vineyards, winemaking traditions, and the rich flavors that define Sicilian wines.

Meeting Point: Palermo City Center

Your wine tasting tour begins in the heart of Palermo, where your guide provides an overview of the experience that awaits. As you embark on your journey, anticipation builds for the flavorful discoveries that lie ahead.

Winery Visit: Sicilian Viticulture

Your first stop is a local winery, where you'll be welcomed by the lush vineyards and the aroma of grapes ripening in the sun. Discover the winemaking process, from cultivation to fermentation, as your guide explains the nuances of Sicilian viticulture.

Cellar Exploration: Unveiling Secrets

Step into the cellar, where rows of barrels and bottles await. Here, your guide provides insights into aging techniques, grape varieties, and the factors that contribute to the unique character of Sicilian wines.

Wine Tasting Experience: Sicilian Varietals

Savor a selection of Sicilian wines, from robust reds to crisp whites. Your guide leads you through a tasting journey, providing tasting notes and information about each wine's origin, characteristics, and food pairings.

Lunch with a View: Gastronomic Delights

Indulge in a leisurely lunch paired with more wines, enjoying regional dishes that complement the flavors of Sicilian wines. As you dine, take in the panoramic views of the surrounding landscape.

Vineyard Walk: Strolling Among the Vines

After lunch, take a stroll through the vineyards, guided by your expert host. Learn about sustainable practices, the importance of terroir, and the harmonious relationship between the land and the wines it produces.

Winery Boutique: Souvenirs and Selections

Visit the winery's boutique, where you can purchase your favorite wines to take home as souvenirs or gifts. Your guide can offer recommendations based on your preferences, ensuring you leave with a piece of Sicilian terroir.

Reflection and Flavorful Memories

As your wine tasting tour comes to a close, take a moment to reflect on the sensory journey you've undertaken. Palermo's wine culture has unfolded before you, revealing the passion and craftsmanship that go into each bottle of Sicilian wine.

Cooking Class and Market Tour

Embark on a gastronomic journey through Palermo's culinary landscape with a cooking class and market tour that immerses you in the vibrant world of Sicilian cuisine. Guided by expert chefs, this experience allows you to explore local markets, select fresh ingredients, and learn the art of creating authentic Sicilian dishes.

Meeting Point: Ballarò Market

Your culinary adventure begins at the bustling Ballarò Market, where your chef guide introduces you to the vibrant array of produce, spices, and ingredients that define Sicilian cuisine. As you navigate the market's lively alleys, anticipation builds for the culinary creations you'll soon prepare.

Ingredient Selection: Market Insights

Accompanied by your chef guide, handpick fresh ingredients for the dishes you'll be preparing during the cooking class. Learn about the significance of seasonal ingredients and the role they play in Sicilian cooking.

Cooking Class: Mastering Sicilian Recipes

Head to the cooking class venue, where your chef instructor guides you through the step-by-step process of creating classic Sicilian dishes. From pasta to seafood specialties, discover the techniques, flavors, and traditions that make Sicilian cuisine unique.

Hands-On Experience: Culinary Artistry

Roll up your sleeves and immerse yourself in the cooking process. Under the guidance of your chef, engage in hands-on preparation, blending ingredients, shaping dough, and infusing each dish with your personal touch.

Wine Pairing: Savoring Sicilian Wines

While your dishes simmer and bake, indulge in a wine tasting experience that pairs Sicilian wines with your upcoming meal. Your chef and sommelier guide you through the art of wine pairing, enhancing your appreciation for the harmonious interplay of flavors.

Dining Delights: Feast on Your Creations

As your dishes reach their culinary peak, gather around the table to savor the fruits of your labor. Enjoy a leisurely meal that showcases the dishes you've prepared, complemented by the expertly selected wines.

Recipe Sharing: Preserving Sicilian Traditions

After the meal, your chef shares the recipes you've prepared, ensuring that the flavors of Sicilian cuisine can be recreated in your own kitchen. Take home not just memories, but also the knowledge to continue your culinary journey.

Reflection and Gastronomic Memories

As you conclude your cooking class and market tour, take a moment to reflect on the culinary adventure you've experienced. The market's bustling energy, the camaraderie of the cooking class, and the flavors of your creations have all contributed to a memorable and enriching day.

DAY TRIPS

Palermo, with its rich history, stunning architecture, and vibrant culture, serves as a perfect base for exploring the diverse landscapes and attractions that Sicily has to offer. From ancient ruins to charming coastal towns, here are some outstanding day trip options that will enrich your Palermo experience:

Cefalù

Nestled along the northern coast of Sicily, Cefalù is a charming town renowned for its stunning natural beauty, historical significance, and relaxed atmosphere. This coastal gem is situated approximately an hour's drive east of Palermo, making it an easily accessible and rewarding destination for a day trip.

Historical Significance: Cefalù Cathedral

The centerpiece of Cefalù is its awe-inspiring cathedral, formally known as the Cathedral-Basilica of Cefalù. This masterpiece of Norman architecture dates back to the 12th century and is a UNESCO World Heritage Site. The cathedral's exterior showcases intricate details and ornate decorations, while its interior boasts impressive mosaics that depict biblical scenes and stories. The fusion of architectural styles, including Norman, Byzantine, and Arab influences, makes the cathedral a captivating example of the cultural diversity that has shaped Sicily's history.

Quaint Streets and Coastal Views

Wandering through Cefalù's narrow, winding streets is a delightful experience. The town exudes a relaxed and welcoming atmosphere, inviting visitors to explore its historic alleys, quaint shops, and charming cafes. As you stroll through the streets, you'll likely come across vibrant squares where locals and visitors gather to enjoy the ambiance. Cefalù's coastal location offers breathtaking views of the Tyrrhenian Sea. The town's golden sandy beach is a popular spot for relaxation and sunbathing. Whether you choose to bask in the sun, take a leisurely swim, or simply enjoy the view, the beach provides a serene escape from the hustle and bustle of daily life.

La Rocca: A Panoramic Adventure

For those seeking a bit of adventure and panoramic vistas, a hike up to La Rocca, a rocky promontory that overlooks Cefalù, is a must. The hike takes you through a scenic path surrounded by lush vegetation and ancient ruins. Upon reaching the summit, you'll be rewarded with sweeping views of the town, the coastline, and the surrounding landscape—a perfect vantage point for capturing memorable photographs.

Culinary Delights

Cefalù is also known for its culinary offerings. Seafood lovers will find a plethora of restaurants serving freshly caught fish and other local delicacies. Dining by the sea, with the sound of waves and the refreshing sea breeze, adds to the overall dining experience.

Monreale

Nestled on a hillside overlooking Palermo, Monreale is a small town that boasts a remarkable treasure – the Monreale Cathedral. This cathedral, along with its breathtaking mosaics and architectural splendor, attracts visitors from all corners of the world.

Monreale Cathedral: A Masterpiece of Mosaics

The Monreale Cathedral, officially known as the Cathedral of Santa Maria Nuova, is a sublime fusion of Norman, Byzantine, and Arab architectural influences. Its construction was commissioned by William II in the 12th century, showcasing the intricate craftsmanship of the period. However, the cathedral's true masterpiece lies within its walls – the extraordinary mosaics that adorn the interior. The mosaics of Monreale Cathedral are a sight to behold, covering nearly 68,000 square feet of surface area. These mosaics depict intricate scenes from the Bible, showcasing stories from the Old and New Testaments in vivid detail. The use of gold leaf and a rich color palette creates a mesmerizing interplay of light and color that fills the cathedral with an ethereal atmosphere.

Exploring the Cathedral Complex

Adjacent to the cathedral is the Cloister of Monreale, an architectural gem in its own right. The cloister features 228 intricate columns, each adorned with unique patterns and designs. It provides a serene setting for contemplation and reflection, with lush gardens and a tranquil ambiance that contrasts the grandeur of the cathedral.

Wandering Through Monreale

Beyond the cathedral complex, Monreale offers visitors a chance to immerse themselves in its charming streets and local life. The town's medieval architecture, cobblestone alleys, and quaint squares evoke a sense of timelessness. Exploring these streets provides insights into the local culture and a chance to interact with friendly residents.

Panoramic Views and Beyond

For panoramic views of Monreale and the surrounding landscape, visitors can ascend the nearby Rocca di Monreale. This vantage point provides a sweeping vista that extends from the town to the shimmering waters of the Tyrrhenian Sea.

A Culmination of Culture

Monreale's historical and artistic significance is truly a culmination of various cultures and influences that have shaped Sicily's history. The fusion of Norman, Byzantine, and Arab elements in its architecture and mosaics stands as a testament to the region's diverse heritage.

Agrigento

Situated on the southern coast of Sicily, Agrigento stands as a testament to the glory of ancient Greek civilization. This remarkable town is home to the Valley of the Temples, an archaeological site of immense historical and cultural significance.

Valley of the Temples: A Glimpse into Antiquity

The Valley of the Temples, a UNESCO World Heritage Site, offers a mesmerizing glimpse into the past, transporting visitors to a time when the city of Akragas (modern-day Agrigento) was a thriving Greek colony. This archaeological park houses a collection of well-preserved Doric temples and structures that stand as a testament to the architectural prowess and artistic vision of the ancient Greeks. Among the prominent temples, the Temple of Concordia stands out as an iconic example of ancient Greek temple design. Its remarkably preserved columns and intricate details showcase the harmonious proportions that characterize Doric architecture. The Temple of Hera, dedicated to the goddess of marriage and childbirth, also boasts impressive remains that give insight into ancient religious practices.

Archaeological Marvels and the Ancient City

Beyond the temples, the Valley of the Temples features an array of ruins, including the remains of city walls, necropolises, and other structures that provide a comprehensive understanding of daily life in ancient Akragas.

Agrigento's Old Town: A Blend of History and Charm

Agrigento's historical significance extends beyond the Valley of the Temples. The town itself offers a captivating blend of history and charm. The Old Town features medieval architecture, narrow streets, and charming squares, providing a delightful atmosphere for exploration. The Cathedral of San

Gerlando, with its mix of architectural styles, stands as a focal point of the town.

Agrigento's Almond Blossom Festival

For those fortunate enough to visit in late winter or early spring, Agrigento's Almond Blossom Festival offers a unique cultural experience. This vibrant festival celebrates the blooming almond trees that paint the landscape with shades of white and pink. Traditional music, dance, and local delicacies contribute to the festive atmosphere.

Segesta

Nestled in the picturesque landscapes of western Sicily, Segesta is an archaeological treasure that offers a captivating journey into the world of ancient Greek architecture and culture.

The Temple of Segesta: A Triumph of Doric Architecture

The highlight of Segesta is undoubtedly the Temple of Segesta, an architectural marvel that stands as a testament to the ingenuity of ancient Greek builders. This remarkably well-preserved Doric temple stands atop a hill, surrounded by rolling hills and green landscapes. The temple's harmonious proportions and graceful columns exemplify the purity of Doric architectural style. Unlike many other ancient sites, the Temple of Segesta was never completed, allowing us a unique glimpse into the construction techniques of the time. The temple's serene setting and its integration with the natural surroundings create an awe-inspiring atmosphere that transports visitors to the world of ancient Greece.

The Segesta Theater: An Acoustic Marvel

Adjacent to the temple is the Segesta Theater, another testament to the advanced architectural knowledge of the ancient inhabitants. Carved into the hillside, this well-preserved theater offers not only historical insight but also an exceptional acoustic experience. The theater's design, with its impeccable seating arrangement and finely tuned acoustics, allows even a whisper on stage to be heard clearly throughout the auditorium.

Wandering Through History and Nature

Exploring Segesta goes beyond the temple and theater. The surrounding landscape provides ample opportunities for hiking and exploration. A walk to the top of the hill offers panoramic views of the temple, theater, and the sweeping countryside—a rewarding experience that enriches the historical visit.

Cultural Significance and Historical Context

Segesta was established by the indigenous Elymian people and was later occupied by the ancient Greeks. This blend of cultures is reflected in the architectural styles and artifacts found in the area. The historical context of Segesta's development adds depth to the experience, providing insight into the interactions and influences that shaped the region.

Erice

Perched high on a mountain overlooking the city of Trapani and the Tyrrhenian Sea, Erice is a captivating destination that beckons travelers with its medieval charm and breathtaking panoramas.

Medieval Architecture and Atmosphere

Erice's cobblestone streets, ancient walls, and well-preserved buildings evoke a sense of stepping back in time. The town's medieval character is beautifully preserved, offering visitors a chance to immerse themselves in a world of historical wonder. The architecture reflects the diverse influences that have shaped Sicily's history, including Norman, Arab, and Spanish elements.

Venus Castle:

At the heart of Erice stands the iconic Venus Castle (Castello di Venere), which dates back to the Norman era. This fortress offers not only historical insights but also unparalleled views of the surrounding landscape. As you wander through the castle's ruins, you'll be rewarded with panoramic vistas that stretch from the coastline to the hills.

Charming Streets and Delightful Shops

Exploring Erice's streets is a delight in itself. Quaint shops, artisan workshops, and charming cafes line the narrow alleyways, creating a picturesque and inviting atmosphere. Local handicrafts, including ceramics and traditional pastries, provide unique souvenirs to take home.

Erice's Religious Sites

Erice is also home to several churches and religious sites that reflect the town's spiritual significance. The Chiesa Matrice, Erice's main church, boasts a mix of architectural styles and stunning artwork. The Church of San Martino, with its Gothic features, offers a serene space for reflection.

Scientific and Culinary Exploration

Erice is not only known for its historical and architectural riches but also for its scientific contributions. The Ettore

Majorana Foundation and Centre for Scientific Culture is an international hub for scientific research and conferences, underscoring Erice's modern importance. Culinary enthusiasts will find delight in Erice's traditional pastries and sweets. The town is renowned for its marzipan creations, often shaped into intricate designs that reflect its rich cultural heritage.

Trapani

Nestled along the western coast of Sicily, Trapani is a captivating town that seamlessly blends its rich historical heritage with its coastal beauty. This coastal gem offers an array of attractions, from ancient landmarks to scenic vistas and bustling markets.

Historical Landmarks and Architecture

Trapani's historical significance is evident in its architectural wonders. The town's historic center boasts Baroque and medieval architecture that showcases the region's diverse influences. The Church of Purgatory (Chiesa del Purgatorio) with its intricate sculptures and the Cathedral of San Lorenzo, a blend of styles from Gothic to Baroque, stand as testament to Trapani's artistic heritage.

Egadi Islands: A Seafaring Adventure

Trapani serves as a gateway to the stunning Egadi Islands—Favignana, Levanzo, and Marettimo. These islands offer a tranquil escape with crystal-clear waters, hidden coves, and opportunities for snorkeling and diving. The Egadi Islands are a paradise for nature enthusiasts and those seeking a respite from the bustling world.

Salt Flats and Windmills

Trapani's surrounding salt flats have been a vital part of the town's history and economy for centuries. The salt pans are a picturesque sight, with their geometric patterns and iconic windmills. The Museo del Sale (Salt Museum) offers insights into the salt production process and the cultural significance of this trade.

Fish Market and Culinary Delights

Trapani's lively fish market is a must-visit for food enthusiasts. Here, you can witness the daily rhythm of local life as fishermen and vendors offer the freshest catch of the day. The town's culinary scene revolves around seafood, and traditional dishes like couscous with fish and "cuddiruni," a local street food, showcase the region's flavors.

Ligny Tower: A Historical Sentinel

The Ligny Tower (Torre di Ligny) stands as a historic fortress on the waterfront, offering panoramic views of the sea and town. This tower serves as a reminder of Trapani's maritime past and its strategic importance in the Mediterranean.

Trapani's Festivals and Traditions

Trapani is known for its vibrant festivals that showcase the town's deep-rooted cultural heritage. The Misteri di Trapani, a Good Friday procession, is a remarkable event where massive statues depicting scenes from the Passion of Christ are paraded through the streets. This tradition reflects the town's strong connection to its religious and artistic history.

Selinunte

Nestled along the Mediterranean coastline, Selinunte stands as a testament to the grandeur of ancient Greek civilization. This remarkable archaeological site is home to a stunning array of ruins, including majestic temples, that transport visitors to a time of architectural brilliance and cultural significance.

Temples of Selinunte:

The most iconic feature of Selinunte is its impressive temples, which are scattered across the site. The Temples of Selinunte are a collection of Doric-style structures that once served as places of worship and communal gathering for the ancient city of Selinus. The Temple of Hera (Temple E) is particularly remarkable, with its massive size and impressive columns that reach towards the sky. This temple, dedicated to the goddess Hera, offers a glimpse into the scale and magnificence of ancient Greek architecture.

Acropolis and Ruins:

Exploring Selinunte allows visitors to immerse themselves in the history and daily life of the ancient city. The Acropolis, a fortified area on a hill overlooking the sea, was a strategic and cultural center. As you stroll through the ruins of temples, city walls, and dwellings, you can almost hear the echoes of the past, imagining the vibrant city that once thrived here.

Archaeological Park and Museum

Selinunte's archaeological park provides a comprehensive experience for history enthusiasts. The park is thoughtfully designed to guide visitors through the various sections of the site, allowing you to explore at your own pace. The adjacent archaeological museum offers a wealth of artifacts, including sculptures, pottery, and tools, that provide insights into the lives of the people who inhabited the area.

Coastal Beauty and Scenic Views

Selinunte's coastal location enhances its allure. The shimmering waters of the Mediterranean Sea create a serene backdrop for the ancient ruins, adding to the poetic ambiance of the site. The nearby beach offers a refreshing break, allowing you to bask in the sun and enjoy the sound of the waves.

Cultural Significance and Exploration

Selinunte's history is richly intertwined with the broader cultural tapestry of ancient Greece and the Mediterranean world. The site's location contributed to its interactions with other civilizations, leaving behind a legacy that goes beyond its architectural wonders.

Marsala

Nestled along the western coast of Sicily, Marsala is a town with a rich tapestry of history, a deep connection to winemaking, and a coastal allure that captivates visitors.

Historical Landmarks and Architecture

Marsala's historical significance is evident in its architecture and landmarks. The town's historic center is a charming maze of narrow streets, baroque churches, and elegant palaces that reflect the region's diverse cultural influences. The Cathedral of Saint Thomas of Canterbury and the Church of Purgatory (Chiesa del Purgatorio) stand as historical and architectural treasures that offer insights into Marsala's past.

Marsala Wine: A World-Famous Elixir

Marsala is internationally renowned for its namesake wine, which has been produced here for centuries. The town's wineries and cellars offer a glimpse into the winemaking process, from grape cultivation to the aging of the prized Marsala wine. Wine enthusiasts can partake in tastings and learn about the traditions that have made Marsala wine a symbol of the region's viticultural heritage.

Mozia: An Archaeological Gem

Just off the coast of Marsala lies the ancient island of Mozia (Mothia). This archaeological site offers a journey into the past, with ruins that tell the story of a Phoenician settlement. The island's museum showcases artifacts recovered from excavations and sheds light on the island's historical significance.

Salt Flats and Windmills

Marsala's salt flats are another emblematic feature of the town's landscape. The geometric patterns of salt pans and the iconic windmills create a picturesque scene that highlights the town's connection to salt production, an industry that has played a pivotal role in its history.

Coastal Charm and Cuisine

Marsala's coastal setting adds to its allure. The town's waterfront promenade provides a pleasant place to stroll and enjoy sea views. Marsala's culinary scene is a treat for the senses, with seafood dishes and traditional Sicilian flavors taking center stage. Seafood restaurants along the coast allow visitors to savor the freshest catches while embracing the refreshing sea breeze.

Egadi Islands

The Egadi Islands—Favignana, Levanzo, and Marettimo—are a trio of enchanting islands that beckon travelers with their pristine landscapes, azure waters, and a sense of tranquility that is often found in secluded paradises.

Favignana: The Butterfly Island

Favignana, the largest of the Egadi Islands, boasts a unique shape resembling a butterfly, with two sweeping bays forming its wings. The island is celebrated for its inviting beaches, such as Cala Rossa and Lido Burrone, where visitors can bask in the sun and swim in the crystalline waters. A network of bicycle paths makes exploring the island's charming villages and coastal vistas a delight. The old tuna factory, Tonnara di Favignana, offers insights into the island's historical tuna fishing industry.

Levanzo: A Tranquil Escape

Levanzo is the smallest of the Egadi Islands, known for its tranquil atmosphere and stunning landscapes. The island's unspoiled beauty is best appreciated by exploring its walking trails, secluded coves, and the famous Grotta del Genovese, a cave adorned with prehistoric rock art that provides a glimpse into ancient human history.

Marettimo: A Natural Haven

Marettimo, the most remote of the Egadi Islands, is a true haven for nature lovers. Its rugged coastline, hidden coves, and diverse marine life make it a paradise for snorkeling and diving. The island's quaint village exudes an authentic Sicilian charm, while hiking trails reveal breathtaking vistas of the sea and the mainland.

Crystal-Clear Waters and Marine Life

The Egadi Islands are renowned for their crystal-clear waters that reveal a vibrant underwater world. Snorkelers and divers will be rewarded with the sight of colorful fish, intricate coral formations, and underwater caves. The islands' marine protected area ensures the preservation of these treasures for generations to come.

Cultural and Culinary Richness

Beyond their natural beauty, the Egadi Islands boast a rich cultural heritage. Local traditions, such as fishing and boat building, provide a glimpse into the islands' history. Culinary delights await visitors, with fresh seafood being a highlight of the local cuisine.

ITINERARIES

Here are ten diverse itineraries to explore the enchanting city of Palermo. Each itinerary offers a unique perspective on the city's history, culture, architecture, and culinary delights.

Historical Marvels and Cultural Immersion

Day 1-2: Immerse yourself in Palermo's historical center, exploring the Norman Palace, Palermo Cathedral, and the vibrant markets.

Day 3-4: Visit the Capuchin Catacombs, Palazzo dei Normanni, and the Church of San Cataldo.

Day 5-6: Explore the Teatro Massimo and the picturesque streets of the Kalsa district.

Day 7: Relax in Villa Giulia or enjoy a leisurely stroll along the seafront.

Artistic Treasures and Culinary Delights

Day 1-2: Discover the city's artistic side by visiting the Palazzo Abatellis and the Galleria d'Arte Moderna.

Day 3-4: Dive into the street food scene at the Ballarò and Vucciria markets.

Day 5: Explore the Palermo Botanical Garden and enjoy a traditional Sicilian meal.

Day 6-7: Visit the Museum of Contemporary Art and take a cooking class to learn Sicilian recipes.

Architecture and Ancient Sites

Day 1-2: Explore the iconic Norman Palace, the Palatine Chapel, and the Cathedral of Palermo.

Day 3-4: Discover the ancient ruins of Solunto and Segesta on day trips from Palermo.

Day 5-6: Visit the Oratory of San Lorenzo and the Zisa Castle.

Day 7: Marvel at the city's architecture, from the Art Nouveau villas to the modern structures.

Palermo by Night

Day 1-2: Spend your evenings at local trattorias and experience the city's nightlife.

Day 3-4: Explore the charming alleys and squares of the historic center during the day.

Day 5-6: Enjoy an opera performance at the Teatro Massimo and savor a late-night gelato.

Day 7: Experience the lively atmosphere of the Ballarò market in the evening.

Gardens and Relaxation

Day 1-2: Visit the Villa Bonanno and Villa Giulia gardens for relaxation and sightseeing.

Day 3-4: Explore the serene Orto Botanico and the lush Parco della Favorita.

Day 5-7: Take leisurely strolls through the city's parks and gardens, enjoying moments of tranquility.

Religious Heritage and Spiritual Exploration

Day 1-2: Begin with a visit to the Cathedral of Palermo and the Church of San Cataldo.

Day 3-4: Explore the Capuchin Catacombs and the historic churches of the city.

Day 5: Participate in a guided religious tour to learn about the city's spiritual significance.

Day 6-7: Spend time in quiet reflection at local churches and enjoy the spiritual ambiance.

Architecture and Modern Art

Day 1-2: Explore Palermo's architectural gems, including the Teatro Massimo and the Quattro Canti.

Day 3-4: Visit contemporary art galleries and museums, such as the Palazzo Riso.

Day 5-6: Experience Palermo's modern side by observing its evolving urban landscape.

Day 7: Take a guided architectural tour to delve deeper into the city's design.

Palermo's Seaside Charm

Day 1-2: Begin with a visit to the seafront promenade and Castello a Mare.

Day 3-4: Explore the picturesque Mondello beach and enjoy seafood by the coast.

Day 5-6: Discover the coastal villages of Aspra and Santa Flavia on day trips.

Day 7: Spend a day at the beach, basking in the sun and enjoying the sea breeze.

Market Exploration and Local Flavors

Day 1-2: Dive into the bustling street markets, such as the Ballarò and Capo markets.

Day 3-4: Experience the city's culinary scene through cooking classes and food tours.

Day 5: Visit a local winery for wine tasting and experience the local vineyards.

Day 6-7: Discover hidden trattorias and eateries, savoring traditional Sicilian dishes.

Palermo's Hidden Gems

Day 1-2: Seek out lesser-known sites, like the Oratorio di San Mercurio and Palazzo Chiaramonte.

Day 3-4: Explore the creative district of Kalsa and visit the Casa Professa.

Day 5-6: Discover hidden courtyards and art studios scattered throughout the city.

Day 7: Spend the day exploring Palermo's off-the-beaten-path neighborhoods and local hangouts.

MAPS

City Map

v

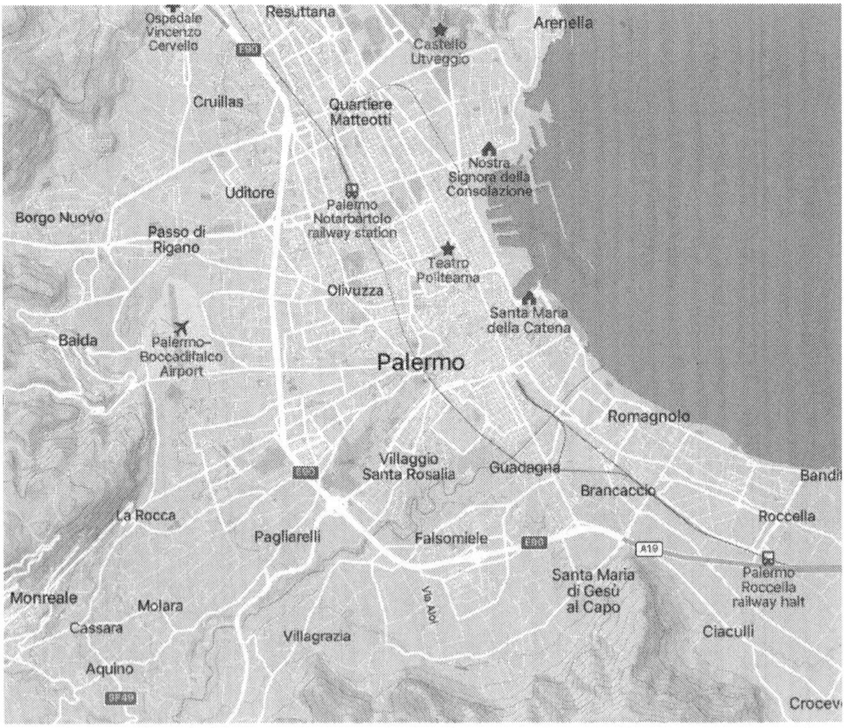

Teatro Massimo Map

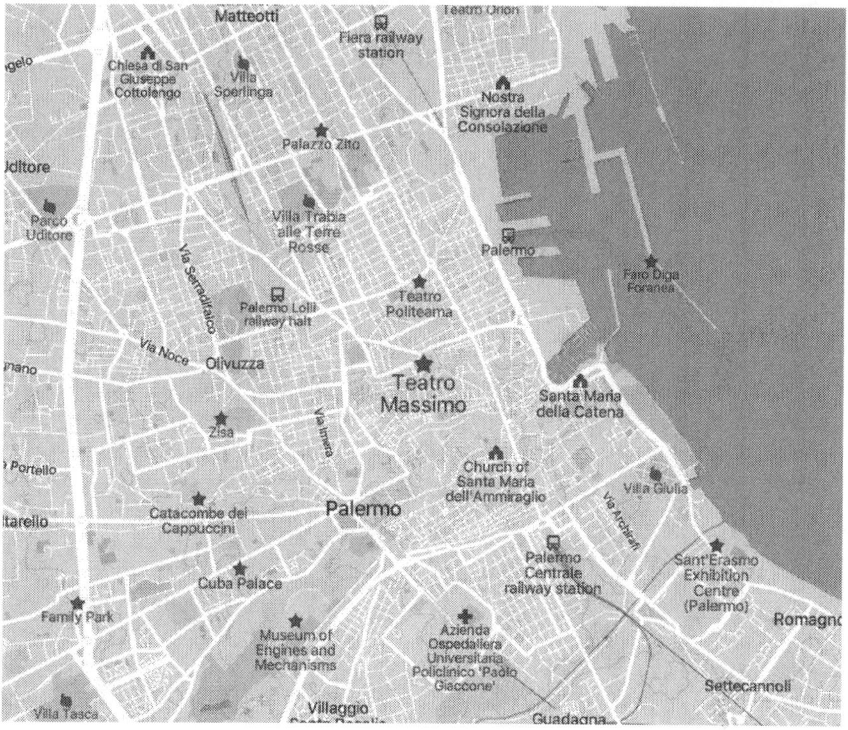

Palermo Cathedral

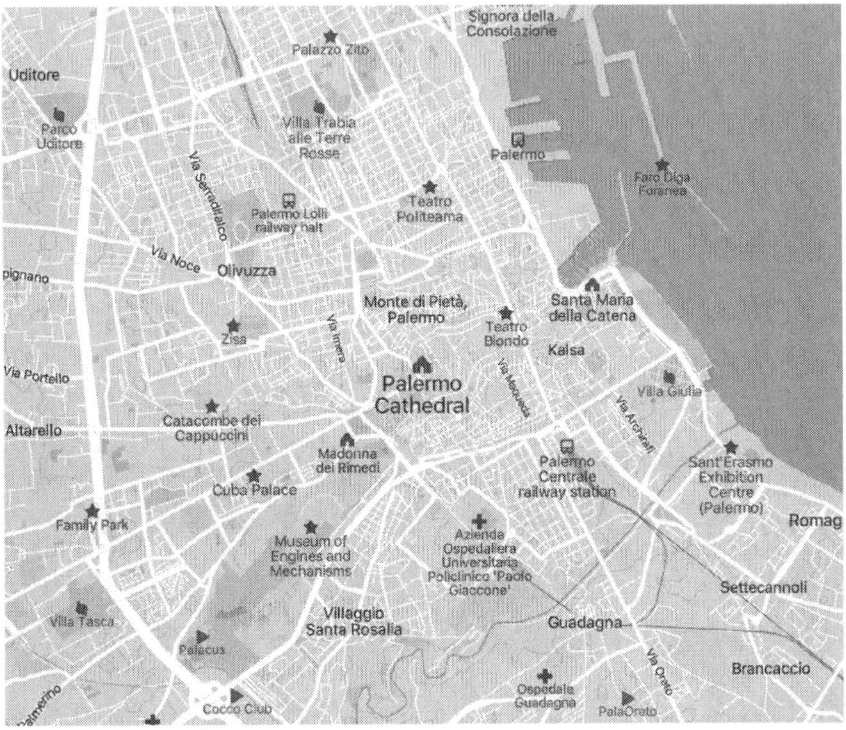

Accommodation Map

Parks and Green Spaces Map

CONCLUSION

As our exploration of Palermo's cultural hub comes to an end, we hope this travel guide has ignited your passion for discovery and fostered a deep connection to the allure of this Sicilian gem. Palermo is more than a destination; it's a journey that invites you to engage with history, embrace diversity, and savor the simple pleasures of life.

Whether you've marveled at the grandeur of Palermo's palaces, savored the flavors of its distinctive cuisine, or simply absorbed the energy of its vibrant streets, remember that each moment has enriched the fabric of your journey. As you bid farewell to this city, carry with you the memories of its vibrant markets, the echoes of its historic sites, and the spirit of a place that cherishes tradition while embracing the future.

May the colors, scents, and sounds of Palermo continue to inspire your travels. The memories you've gathered here will remain a source of inspiration, guiding you back whenever you yearn for the charm of its streets, the authenticity of its culture, and the heartwarming embrace of its people. Until we meet again, let the spirit of Palermo accompany you on your future adventures and remind you of the beauty that can be found in every corner of the world.

INDEX

Accommodation in Palermo 14

Accommodation Map 164

Agrigento 146

Albergheria 28

Ancient Roots and Early Settlers 18

Arab-Norman Architecture98

Architecture and Ancient Sites 157

Architecture and Modern Art 159

Art and Architecture Tour 130

Artistic Expressions 99

Artistic Treasures and Culinary Delights 157

Ballarò Market 123

Baroque Architecture 96

Basic Information 10

Beaches and Coastal Beauty in Palermo 103

Breathtaking Sunset spots 117

Byzantine and Arab Influences 20

Camping under the Sicilian Sky 112

Cantieri Culturali alla Zisa 59

Capo 30

Capo Market 124

Cappella Palatina 68

Castello di Cefalà Diana 50

Catacombe dei Cappuccini (Capuchin Catacombs) 42

Cattedrale di Palermo 66

Cefalù 143

Church of Saint John of the Hermits 76

City Map 161

Contemporary Palermo 25

Cooking Class and Market Tour 140

Countryside Horseback Riding 111

Egadi Islands155

Erice 149

Etnografico Siciliano Museum 61

FAQ 15

Fontana Pretoria (Pretoria Fountain) 48

Gardens and Oases in Palermo 105

Gardens and Relaxation 158

Giuseppe verdi statue 89

Hiking in the Zingaro Nature Reserve 111

Historical Marvels and Cultural Immersion 157

Historical Walking Tour 127

Kalsa-Marina 32

Kayaking along Sicily's Coastline 111

La Cuba 45

La Kalsa 26

La Loggia District 34

La Martorana 73

Mafia History Tour 137

Market Exploration and Local Flavors 159

Marsala 153

Modern Art at GAM Palermo 64

Monreale 145

Mountain Biking in the Madonie Mountains 110

Mountain Hikes in Palermo 102

Museo Archeologico Regionale 55

Museo delle Maioliche Stanze al Genio 58

Museo Internazionale delle Marionette Antonio Pasqualino 56

National Parks in Palermo 107

Nature Reserves in Palermo 106

Nighttime Ghost Tour 132

Norman Cathedral of Palermo 40

Norman Conquest and Cultural Fusion 21

Oratorio di San Lorenzo 71

Palazzo Abatellis 62

Palazzo dei Normanni (Palace of the Normans) 36

Palazzo dei Normanni District 33

Palazzo dei Normanni Museum 54

Palermo Bike Tour 133

Palermo by Night 158

Palermo Cathedral 163

Palermo's Hidden Gems 160

Palermo's Seaside Charm 159

Parks and Green Spaces Map 165

Port of Palermo 12

Quattro Canti (Four Corners) 38

Religious Heritage and Spiritual Exploration 158

Rock Climbing at Monte Pellegrino 111

Sailing in the Tyrrhenian Sea 112

San Giovanni degli Eremiti 69

Santuario Santa Rosalia 72

Segesta 148

Segway Tour 135

Selinunte 152

Snorkeling and Diving in Isola delle Femmine 111

Spanish Domination and Baroque Splendor 22

Statue of Carlo V 79

Statue of Giuseppe Garibaldi 82

Statue of Ruggero Settimo 80

Statue of Saint Francis of Paola 91

Statue of Santa Rosalia 85

Statue of the Genius of Palermo (Il Genio di Palermo) 84

Statue of Vincenzo Florio 87

Street Food 121

Street Food Tour 128

Teatro Massimo 39

Teatro Massimo Map 162

The Opera 95

The Palatine Chapel 74

Trapani 150

Unification of Italy and Modernization 23

Vibrant Markets 119

Villa palagonia 52

Vucciria 29

Vucciria Market 46

Water activities 113

Wildlife in Palermo 108

Wine Tasting Tour 139

Zisa Palace 43

Printed in Great Britain
by Amazon

27723220R00134